COMPLETELY REVISED AND UPDATED

THE BUSY EDUCATOR GUIDE TO THE WORLD WIDE WEB

Marjan Glavac

NIMA Systems
London, Ontario,
Canada
http://www.glavac.com

NIMA Systems
509 Commissioners Rd., W., Suite 317
LONDON, Ontario, Canada N6J 1Y5
http://www.glavac.com

Discounts of 30% off available for orders of 10 books or more. Other significant discounts are available for educational fundraising, (home and school, student council, fun fairs etc.) business, or promotional use. E-mail **marjan@glavac.com** for more details.

Canadian Cataloguing in Publication Data

Glavac, Marjan, 1955-
    The busy educator's guide to the world wide web

Completely rev. and updated 2nd ed.
Includes bibliographical references and index.
ISBN 0-9683310-1-7

    1. World Wide Web (Information retrieval system).
2. Internet (Computer network) in education. 3. Teaching--
Computer network resources. I. Title

LB1044.87.G59 2000   025.06'37   C00-901111-0

Every reasonable effort has been made to obtain permission for all articles and data used in this book. If errors or omissions have occurred, the author or publisher will update information received in subsequent editions or on the website: **http://www.glavac.com**

Credits

Editor Maria Skale
Cover and Art Kathy Hayes
Otabind Printing Webcom Limited

To Stu Cunningham, a master principal, educator and leader
who taught me all about risk taking,
"pats on the back" and
asking my students everyday before lunch and hometime,
"what did you learn today?"

Read What They Said About Marjan Glavac's
The Busy Educator's Guide To The World Wide Web 1st. Ed.

"Marjan Glavac, a veteran educator and winner of numerous national awards, has created a vital tool in 'The Busy Educator's Guide To The World Wide Web'. His years of successful use of the web and the Internet in the classroom have enabled him to sift through thousands of web resources and document the very best of the best. This guide will prove invaluable to any teacher who uses the web in the classroom."

Caroline McCullen Technology & Learning 1996 National Teacher of the Year
Instructional Technologist SAS Institute, SAS Campus Drive, Cary, NC 27513, USA
MidLink Magazine http://longwood.cs.ucf.edu/~MidLink

"When the students of today graduate into the 21st century, they will arrive into an economy and society that is increasingly wired together - and which is unlike anything that has come before. It is critical that they be provided the outlook, skills, motivation, and awareness that will allow them to make the right decisions with respect to their careers - and indeed, their future. That's why this book can be so useful -- it provides to the teacher some of the background, insight, and resources that can be used to best discover the Internet, and maximize its potential for use within the classroom."

Jim Carroll, C.A. Coauthor of the *Canadian Internet Handbook* www.jimcarroll.com

"I know how busy teachers are and I know how important it is for modern teachers to use the Internet. This book will be of invaluable assistance to busy teachers who need to get on the net."

John Ramsay Former Head of English Centennial S.S. Welland, Ontario, Canada
Author of *Public Lives Private Voices* Oxford University Press of Canada

"This is the book for teachers who want to find engaging Internet resources and activities to use with their students. There is something for everybody!"

Diane Midness, Project Coordinator International School Partnerships through Technology
North Carolina Center for International Understanding
Dmidness@mindspring.com
http://www.mindspring.com/~dmidness   http://www.ga.unc.edu/NCCIU/ispt

"What every teacher needs to know in order to travel the Information Highway."

Edith Jacobson Economics Teacher
Garfield High School, Los Angeles, California, USA

"Includes comprehensive, informative, and easy-to-understand search strategies and techniques."

Kathleen Schrock, MLS author of *Kathy Schrock's Guide for Educators*
http://www.capecod.net/schrockguide/
Technology Coordinator Dennis-Yarmouth Regional School District S.Yarmouth MA, USA

"Be proactive in your teaching. Use the chapters of this book to extend your students' horizons. Let them act locally and think globally."

Bernie Beswick BSc. MEd. Teacher, Loganlea State High School, Australia

"Original and succinct. A wonderful educational tool. The 'Sites That Motivate, Engage And Stimulate Students And Educators' chapter is an excellent reference source, providing a breadth and depth of essential educational information."

David Shaw Junior School Computers Newcastle Grammar School Newcastle NSW Australia

"In the traveling through cyberspace a busy educator needs to find their way quickly and efficiently. Here is your ticket."

Josh Schwartz Summit Middle School
Tech Lab 2000 Instructor Frisco, Colorado, USA

"Educators of the 21st Century need to know the Web inside and out, for their students' sake... and Marjan Glavac shows them every nook and cranny. Cutting through all the Internet hype, this book enlightens users at all experience levels, giving them tools and resources that they can put to use right away. This is one Internet guide that users will want to keep within arm's reach at all times"

Brian Pomeroy Web Coordinator, Children's Hospital of Philadelphia
Author, "*BeginnerNet: A Beginner's Guide to the Internet and World Wide Web*"

"Marjan Glavac has taken the fear out of surfing the Net. You no longer need to feel like a fly caught on the World Wide Web."

Ann Hounsell, Parent, Bonaventure Meadows Public School, London, Ontario, Canada

"A wonderful resource for those teachers who want to catch up with their students!"

Terry Whitmell , John Fraser SS
Mississauga, Ontario, Canada

"In the comparison between our Interstate Highway System and the Information Superhighway on which the Internet is structured, two differences become evident: the Information Superhighway routes keep changing and there are no signposts identifying the exits on the Internet. Well, this book helps with both - it not only helps one navigate the 'where are we now' but also helps one find short-cuts to the 'next helpful web site'."

Earl J. Moniz Librarian Media Coordinator
Lillington Elementary School Librarian, Lillington, North Carolina, USA

"Learning and the Internet are partners for the future. This guide provides a practical view of how to marry technology and learning for high impact."

Elliott Masie The MASIE Center Saratoga Springs, NY, USA (author and technology futurist)

"Being new to the WWW, I find your chapters more than helpful. I am always looking for good sites and not always finding them on my own. Your book seems to be what I am looking for. Thanks."

Carolyn Leyes,
K-6 Computer Aide at Battell School, Mishawaka, IN, USA

"This was a great opportunity - your writing is great and I learned a lot!"

Karen R. Mensinger library-media specialist
Belfair, WA, USA

"A book from someone who walks the talk. Marjan doesn't just talk Internet; he uses the Internet as an integral part of his classroom program. When he recommends sites, or Internet projects, I take the time to check them out."

Louisa Howerow Teacher Librarian, Jeanne Sauve French Immersion Public School
London, Ontario, Canada

"It is similar in format to other books I've seen but it deals primarily with education. Now we won't have to weed through all kinds of stuff to find what is most beneficial to the classroom. It will be a terrific timesaver."

Patricia F. Mayfield Technology Center/Challenge Grant
Lafayette Parish School Board, Lafayette, Louisiana, USA

"In what I reviewed, it looks to me that this book goes a long way to addressing the problem that teachers have in spending excessive amounts of time trying to find useful Internet resources for student learning. The list of educational sites is excellent and the in-depth description of many sites allows teachers to sort through options more easily."

Mike Seymour, M.S. Director Heritage OnLine http://www.hol.edu
CEO, the Heritage Institute Antioch University, Seattle WA, USA

The book seems ideal for those wishing to learn to use the Internet for its intended purpose- the sharing of information i.e. learning and educating. I can see the book being useful for new Internet users of all ages. In fact I will probably give a copy to my newly Internet- enabled parents because it clearly explains basics such as how the Internet works and, more importantly, how to use it in a useful and effective manner. More experienced users, particularly educators or those looking to use the Internet as a tool for finding or sharing information, will benefit from the book's unique focus on education. Although I've used the Internet for 5 years, I learned several things I didn't know including, for example, the details of how searching engines work not to mention the various useful URL's mentioned throughout."

Michael Chachich, Manager, Referential Data Group, Merrill Lynch, Tokyo, Japan

"This book offers a rich resource of information for educators who are looking for those exceptional, award-winning websites. Topical listings of subject areas are included which offer quick access to what you are looking for as well as suggested grade levels and helpful tips for using these websites in your classroom curriculum are included. This book promises to be a great addition to your collection of educational tips for Internet integration."

Tammy Payton First Grade Teacher and Web-Editor for Loogootee Elementary West
Loogootee, Indiana, USA http://www.siec.k12.in.us/~west/west.htm

"Telecommunications can be an extremely effective curriculum tool for both staff and students. Marjan Glavac's first chapter provides a wealth of information for the busy educator looking for great educational sites. Many of the sites mentioned will help teachers realize that technology should serve pedagogy, not the other way around."

Timothy C. Noxel, Teacher Bluewater Board of Education, Ontario, Canada
Osprey Central Public School, Maxwell, Ontario, Canada

"With the plethora of Internet addresses available to educators in books, journals, CD's, and listservs, it's helpful and timesaving to have a collection of websites 'checked-out', organized, and linked to curricular areas."

Roz Goodman, Media Specialist Southwest Region Schools PO Box 90 Dillingham, AK
bsrlg@aurora.alaska.edu

"Trying to juggle your students, keep the administrators happy, and still learn all about the Internet in your spare time? Buy this book, put your feet up, and you'll feel better in the morning."

Jean Armour Polly, http://www.netmom.com/ Author, *The Internet Kids and Family Yellow Pages,* 2nd Edition Osborne McGraw-Hill (June 1997)

"Any teacher who is about to begin teaching the Internet to his/her students, has taught this discipline for some time, or just wants to know which websites benefit teachers the most needs to have this book on or near their desk as a reference guide. Marjan Glavac's concise descriptions of educational websites and his listing of sites by information and services provided is a definite plus over most books of this nature. As an Internet professional who works in a 'computer tutor' environment with all ages of users, I can appreciate Marjan Glavac's use of easily understood language and lack of technical jargon. Although not considered an educator per se, I'll definitely be adding this book to my reference materials collection."

Brian K. Ross Director, Online Content The Komando Corporation www.komando.com

"Amazing, this is one resource book I wouldn't live without. This book makes it possible to pinpoint REAL SUBSTANCE sites without spending the hours, days and months of searching through link after link of sites that sometimes take you absolutely nowhere. Great gift for the teacher, homeschooler or student in your life. I can't wait to explore all these wonderful sites, thanks so much for such a super resource!"

Gayle Remisch, Homeschooler and Canadian Agent for NASA's K-12 Educational Programs - Passport To Knowledge http://quest.arc.nasa.gov London, Ontario, Canada

"There is a never-ending resource of educational information out there and Mr. Glavac has listed some of the very best for any level of education. I've been fortunate enough to visit some of Mr. Glavac's computer classes. I was very pleased to find that each and every student, whether in grade 2 or grade 6, was so entrenched in what they were learning on the WWW that they hardly noticed someone new in the classroom. They were all learning and really enjoying it. I only wish I'd been born 30 years later and had a teacher like Mr. Glavac!"

Cheryl Smelser, Parent, London, Ontario, Canada

"I have been able to be in a few of Mr.Glavac's classes talking to the students about making money on the Internet. (I helped write reviews for web sites for a New York company writing a book called 'NetKids Rule the Net') The students I spoke to were lucky to have Mr. Glavac as a teacher. They were learning on the Internet and they told me how much they liked it."

Nykki-Lynn Smelser, student, London, Ontario, Canada

About The Author

Marjan Glavac (BA, University of Toronto (St. Michael's College); BEd, Brock University, MA, Carleton University) has used computers in education on the first day he began teaching in 1982. Since 1993, he has introduced thousands of students K-University, parents and teachers to the Internet through online courses, websites, classroom lessons, workshops, speeches, articles, his computer columns for *kidsworld* magazine and his latest book, THE BUSY EDUCATOR'S GUIDE TO THE WORLD WIDE WEB 2ND EDITION.

In 1994 he was a recipient of the Roberta Bondar (first Canadian female astronaut)Award for Science and Technology. In 1995 he won the NORTEL National Institute Award for Excellence in Teaching. He was selected to participate in 3 NORTEL summer institutes. In 1996 he won the Prime Minister's Award for Excellence in Teaching Mathematics, Science and Technology. In 1997, he won the Roy C. Hill Award for educational innovation. In 1998, he was awarded a certificate of merit from TVO (Canadian equivalent to PBS.) In 1998, he also wrote his first book, THE BUSY EDUCATOR'S GUIDE TO THE WORLD WIDE WEB 1ST EDITION.

He and his students have been filmed by TVO and Global's Kids TV, featured in all local media-newspapers, TV and radio, nationally in the *Globe and Mail, Toronto Star, Today's Parent, Home and Educational Computing* and internationally on WGN radio, websites and dozens of student newspapers worldwide.

Marjan has involved his students in projects sponsored by Global SchoolNet Foundation, Kidlink, Academy One, CCCnet, AT&T Japan, Lycos and in the creation of the NewsOntario online newspaper project. K-8 students have also participated in e-mail, travel buddy and research projects with schools all over the world.

He has presented keynotes, workshops and seminars on topics ranging from educational and family software and computer activities to the use of the Internet in the classroom to parents and teachers at international conferences.

His keynote speeches include *Beyond the Rainbow* and *Chalk Board Lessons From The Digital Age* which take the audience on a journey from his first day as a computer fearing teacher to his embracing of "high-tech, high-touch" technology. In a funny and poignant presentation, Marjan shares what inspired him to make his students and school an integral part of the World Wide Web and the Internet.

Marjan is currently a gr. 5 home room teacher at W. Sherwood Fox Public School in London, Ontario, Canada where he resides with his wife Maria and their two children, Vanessa and Collin. He can be contacted by e-mail at **marjan@glavac.com** or through his website at: **http://www.glavac.com**

Foreword

I remember Eric Holden, a brand new middle school teacher, so well. He had been teaching for a month and was totally frustrated in that he wanted suggestions on where to find activities to do in the classroom. The district did not have a new teacher induction program; he did not have a mentor. Basically, he was given a set of textbooks and told to go and teach.

Every new teacher reinvents education all over again. We are a profession entrusted with leaving a legacy for the next generation, yet it is a sad commentary on education that we leave nothing for the next generation of teachers. You would think that a new teacher would be able to find a file full of materials left by past teachers. Instead, we tell new teachers to

Figure it out for yourself,
Do it yourself, and
Keep it to yourself.

I have since heard from Eric and he is doing quite well. What happened? I gave him one or two websites such as:

http://www.new-teacher.com/ (the dash is important)
http://school.discovery.com/schrockguide/index.html

and told him about links. One door opened another, which opened another, and suddenly he had more activities than he knew what to do with.

It took me decades to read magazines and go to conferences before I acquired enough activities for my classroom. Now, with the click of a button, you can find most everything you need.

I still recommend going to conferences and reading certain professional journals. One day I opened "members.aol.com/Jedarling" and found one of the most dignified statements I have ever read on the dignity of teaching. An award-winning English teacher, Judy Darling, wrote two stirring articles

"To All Outstanding Teachers" and *"What Good Teachers Know"*

There is a bright future for those educators who are prepared, are positive, and have added value to their lives. In the blink of an educational eye, the power, the culture, and the future of the teaching profession will reside in the new teachers.

I ask you to access **http://www.new-teacher.com/** This is what new teachers are doing. Like the aforementioned Judy Darling, they are creating their own websites and communicating with each other in a very positive manner. The creator of this web site is 29 years old and is typical of the new breed of teachers people who share and chat with each other. They are supporting and helping each other instantly. You can see leadership exuding from these new teachers. They don't need outdated organizations and negative publications. (One journal even sarcastically gives out awards annually called "Rotten Apple Awards" in their endeavor to help teachers become successful teachers!)

The truly good teachers, new or veteran, have youthful outlooks, energy, optimism, immortality, vision, and the willingness to take risks as their common denominator. They are globally, environmentally, and racially aware. Their sharing on the Internet is how they celebrate the success of schools and teachers.

Education is an institution that thrives, succeeds, and grows on hope, help, sharing, love, and caring. We live in an age where synergies, networks, and collaborations will position individuals and organizations to build connections with those who want to provide a better education and life for our students.

I recommend Marjan Glavac's book to all educators. If you dare to teach, you must never cease to learn. Marjan's book makes the learning process so much faster and rewarding. I hope you enjoy his book and learn and grow from it as much as I have.

Harry K. Wong
orderinfo@harrywong.com

Harry K. Wong, who with his wife Rosemary, are the authors of The First Days of School, which has sold over one million copies.

Contents

Introduction

Ever since a student first showed me how to turn on a computer on my very first day of teaching in September 1982, I have been fascinated by the computer. Over the years, I used it as did many of my colleagues, to integrate it with my class curriculum with varying degrees of success. It was just another tool that we teachers used in the class to make things easier for our students to learn.

Then, in 1990 I saw the potential of the computer as a telecommunications tool. In the basement of our house, my wife was working on a 286 Personal Computer with a software program called Telix, connected to a 2400 baud modem and a telephone line. As I peered over her shoulder, I noticed that she was "chatting" in real time to her colleague miles away in another city. I thought to myself that if she can talk to someone, why can't my students?

Three years later, my students had the opportunity to do just that. The Ontario Teachers' Federation were giving Internet e-mail accounts to any teacher for free. The Canadian government was also offering for free, full Internet service to 300 schools across Canada through the SchoolNet initiative. My school was one of those 300.

That year, the walls of my school came tumbling down. My students were involved in a personal poetry telecommunications project headed by two American teachers, Sheldon Smith of California and Robert Fromme of Texas, with schools from 6 U.S. cities; an Art Ecology exchange project with 28 schools in 5 countries (Canada, USA, Russia, Peru and Japan) and a "Day in Life Project" with over 100 schools in 3 countries. Students used the Internet to exchange e-mail with students in Siberia Russia, Israel and South Carolina, USA. One student used the Canadian government computer to interact in natural language for information on AIDS. Another student downloaded information on UFO sightings in Canada and used this information to plot sightings in Ontario for her Science project. Another student played chess every day with my friend in Saskatoon, Saskatchewan, Canada, and beat him. Something I could never do face to face!

When a student from London, Ontario, Canada can read a poem from a student from San Antonio, Texas, USA and shout spontaneously and exclaim "that person is exactly like me", or when a student from San Antonio, Texas can write back and say "I didn't think anyone would write to me", there lies the power of telecommunications-it's the power to connect and network. Many of my students that year found that students in faraway and diverse states such as California, Illinois, Maryland, Texas, South Carolina and in countries such as Russia and Israel, have a lot in common with them. "They're a lot like us", was a phrase often said by my students.

This technology became even more powerful when I noticed the effect it was having on my special education "at risk" students. These students were overcoming their barriers and communicating with peers of their own age without being prejudiced. The technology freed my students from barriers of sexual, racial and cultural stereotyping. They could communicate a message based on the message itself and not on the way they looked, or what they wore or the way they behaved. My "at risk" students were reading and writing letters, something which they would have had much difficulty doing in the past without a computer and without a purpose. They could now begin to overcome their barriers and connect with peers their own age based on their interests.

The technology has since surpassed in a short time what once I thought would take decades to overcome. Computing costs have decreased dramatically over what they were 5 years ago. More and more schools and homes are now connected to the Internet. With the increase in the number of educators on the Internet, there has been an increase in the information available. The increase in information, has brought the challenge of overcoming information overload.

This book is for every parent, teacher, librarian, administrator-anyone who uses the Internet, and more specifically its graphical tool the World Wide Web to teach children ages 4-18 (K-12). It is for anyone who has experienced information overload trying to use the many resources now available on the Internet. It is also for those educators who already have access to the Internet and the World Wide Web and are comfortable and knowledgeable with the basics of navigating the Internet. It is for those educators who have a vision of giving their students the skills they need to communicate beyond the four walls of their classroom to the world and beyond and who want children to read, write, share, build, communicate and contribute using telecommunications. It is for those who want to do all this, in addition to being in the classroom all day with your students, teaching, dealing with discipline problems, collecting fund raising money, providing extracurricular activities, attending meetings, sending home notes, phoning parents and doing all the necessary "stuff" that makes an educator, an educator. You are the "busy educator" in the book's title.

Disclaimer

This book has been written as a resource for educators. However, the publisher and author are not responsible for the material on the pages referenced by these links. The Internet is a wonderful resource, but information constantly changes and sometimes links that have been deemed "safe" for students, are no longer appropriate. Please use your professional judgement and care when allowing students access to these sites. Although all sites have been checked and re-checked, and chosen on the basis of their educational content and relevance to the classroom, the nature of the Internet is such that changes do occur. Some sites may not be appropriate for certain grades, ages and maturity levels. Try to preview the sites, in advance if possible, just as you would preview a video or any other material before using it in your classroom or with your children.

Please be aware that sometimes you may not be able to access all the links in this book. Visitors could be blocked from entering a site because of routine maintenance, a hardware failure, or because of site traffic. Sites can also move to new locations or become discontinued. If you do encounter problems, try to access the site at another time of day or on a different day of the week. Double check addresses for correct spelling and capitalization.

About This Book

Chapter 1   This chapter is designed to get you using the Internet quickly and efficiently. It gives an overview of top educator, parent and kid's sites on the World Wide Web. If your time is limited, this is a great starting point to access excellent sites.

Chapter 2   A number of great sites are listed in this chapter for teachers who want to find more information on educational standards in their own state, other states and provinces, lesson plan sites, theme sites and sites that provide information for teachers, beginning, substitute and experienced at all grade levels.

Chapter 3   The first pages of this chapter contain links to excellent lessons, tips and strategies to integrate the Internet into your class curriculum. The websites in this chapter are classified according to subjects and grade levels. Grade levels are used here as an estimate only, as abilities among schools and districts vary. The following illustrates the approximate ages of students used with the grade categories:

preschool: (Pre-K) ages 0-3; kindergarten: ages 4-6; grade 1: ages 6-7; grade 2: ages 7-8; grade 3: ages 8-9; grade 4: ages 9-10; grade 5: ages 10-11; grade 6: ages 11-12; grade 7: ages 12-13; grade 8: ages 13-14; grade 9: ages 14-15; grade 10: ages 15-16; grade 11: ages 16-17; grade 12 ages 17-18; College and University: 18+ (grade 16).

Chapter 4   There are an amazing number of great telecommunications projects on the Internet and World Wide Web. This chapter looks at some guidelines for becoming involved in a telecommunications project and some things to know before allowing students to go online. Information is also included on where to find projects, how to keep current with new projects and a description of some notable projects which you may want to do with your students.

Chapter 5   A resource is only valuable if you can access it. This chapter shows you some tips on searching for and finding the information that you and your students need and want. In addition to the well known search engines and directories, there is a list of educational sites, and search engines which have been found to be particularly useful for students and teachers. There is also a chart by Debbie Abilock on how to choose a search engine.

Chapter 6   Reg Ferland, my French instructor at Brock University Teacher's College, often gave us "newbie" teachers in training the following advice: "don't reinvent the wheel". With the widespread use of the Internet, there are a lot of teachers who have shared their resources, experiences and expertise with the world wide educational community. This chapter illustrates how you can share your resources with anyone by using your own website, and where you can find additional resources on the Internet to develop and create your own website.

Appendix   In the appendix is a directory of all the web addresses listed in the book (except for individual listservs found on the AskERIC site). This appendix is designed to help the busy educator sort through sites and information quickly.

Index The index has been designed again with the busy educator in mind. You will see an emphasis on activities, grades, lessons, and subjects and search tools.

The success of the Internet and the World Wide Web has been based on individuals willing to share and collaborate with others. If you have any favorite sites, projects, tips, strategies, ideas or updates to any sites in this book that you would like to share with others, please e-mail them to me at **marjan@glavac.com** I'll post them in my free newsletter or on our website at:
http://www.glavac.com

Two roads diverged in a wood, and I--
I took the one less traveled by,
And that has made all the difference.

Robert Frost

Chapter 1

How To Use The Internet...Real Fast

"The adjustment to the new contexts is where the work is, not in learning the new technology."

Prof. Jerrold Maddox

What has always attracted me to the Internet has been the dizzying pace of change. Just when I've thought that I've discovered the latest and best educational website, the collective and creative community of the Internet always manages to offer even more and better sites. It is in this ever changing atmosphere that sites which maintain their creativity, offer viewers value for their time and strive to engage their audience in interactive forums and discussion groups, are rewarded by our repeat visits.

I have a rule to determine good educational sites for teachers: will they make my teaching easier or harder? The truly great sites offer teachers help in understanding how to implement this new communications technology into the classroom and developing a curriculum which will prepare kids for the next millennium. It's a challenging goal for many sites which bill themselves as educational. Unfortunately the Internet landscape is dotted with haystacks of educational information and resources. The best sources are as elusive as the proverbial needle. Many of the sites tend to offer links to more links with little or no explanation on the links or how the information can be used in the classroom. The viewer is often confronted with information overload. Great educational sites are few and far between. They vary tremendously. Some fit the neat easy to follow magazine type format of parent and kids sites. Some are subject specific, some are grade specific, some are project specific!

The following sites however, do follow my rule. They have helped make my teaching easier and given my students and others an exciting addition to their curriculum. They tend to inform rather than overwhelm. They are worth the most precious commodity a teacher has...time.

Top Educator Sites

A to Z Teacher Stuff
http://atoZTeacherStuff.com/

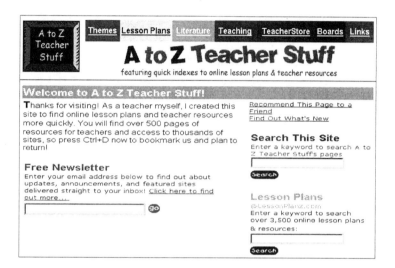

This one-stop resource provides a variety of teaching resources for the online educator. Created by a teacher, it features quick and easy access to thousands of online resources. Find original lesson plans for grades pre-K-12, thematic units and theme resources, teacher tips, educational articles, children's literature activities, top educational sites, and teaching materials. Although the site is extensive, it has a search feature to help you find what you need. Educators can also interact with others on the message boards, or join a collaborative project.

The Theme section is attractively displayed in chart form. Categories featured here include: New Themes and Recent Updates, Seasonal/Holidays, Social Studies, Language Arts/Literature, Science/Health, Math and Misc. Themes. A lot of unique themes here that teachers will really appreciate!

The Lesson Section contains over 175 original lessons submitted by teachers which can be browsed by grade level K-12, new lesson plans, all lesson plans or by lesson plan contributors. A search engine is available to search over 3,500 lesson plans. You can also search them by subject area. Each subject area is further divided into grade categories for easy searching. Teachers won't want to miss the Worksheets and Printable Pages category. Great resources here.

Other sections that teachers would want to check out are the Teaching section featuring A to Z Teacher Tips, and Educational Sites for Teachers.

This is a one stop resource area that you can productively spend your time.

About.com
http://about.com/

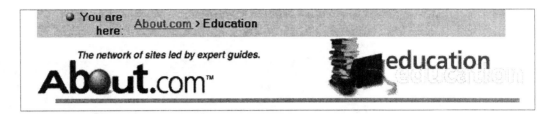

About.com is a vast collection of topic specific sites divided into 28 categories. These categories house over 700 sites. Each site at About.com is consistent in design and function, and led by an About.com Guide. This guide is a dedicated individual who has been hand-picked to provide the best, well-rounded Internet experience in each area of interest.

The education category contains the following subtopics: Adult/Continuing Education, Arts, College/University, History, Languages, Literature, Philosophy/Religion, Primary/Secondary Education, Sciences -- Life/Earth, Sciences --Physical/Computer and Social Sciences.

Currently under the subtopic of Primary/Secondary Education, there are 11 guides offering the following educational sites: Crafts for Kids, Early Childhood Educators, Elementary School Educators, Elementary School Educators: Canada, Homeschooling, Homework Help, Kids' Pen Pals, Math for Kids, Private Schools, Secondary School Educators and Special Education.

The Elementary School Educators site provides educators with the following subjects: Free Lesson Plans, Arts and Crafts, Becoming a Teacher, Classroom Management, Computers/Technical, Departments of Education (US), Early Childhood Education, Finding Freebies, Help for Parents, Homework Helpers, How to Find a Job, How to Substitute, Language Arts, Literature, Mathematics, Multicultural Education, Music and Theater, New Teachers, Physical Education and Health, Science, Social Studies, Special Education, Assessment, Organizations, Books, Educational Games, Geography, Gifted/Talented, Languages and the Millennium.

There are also two other noteworthy sections on this site: the In the Spotlight section highlights an educational Internet site, a seasonal theme and a teacher tool of the week. The Essentials section contains a Teacher Message Board, Free Chalk Talk Newsletter, How To's for Teachers, Hot Education Headlines, Holiday Lesson Plans, Education Chat Room, and Free Lesson Plans. Teacher feedback is encouraged. Bookmark this site and check in once a week.

ACTDEN
http://www.actden.com/

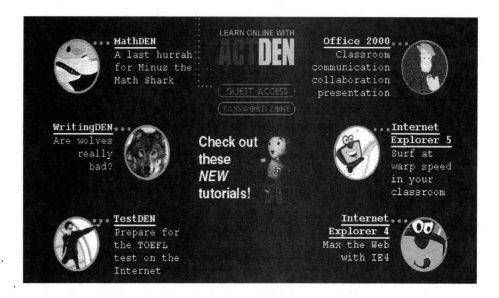

The ACTDEN site is made up of seven DENs or subject categories. Each offers information and interactive features that encourage students to learn and to think:

MathDEN - presents challenging math problems.

WritingDEN - teaches students how to write effectively.

NewsDEN - presents current events in exciting new ways.

GraphicsDEN - introduces students to cool digital art.

SkyDEN- offers a visually stunning introduction to basic astronomy.

InternetDEN - shows teachers how to use Internet Explorer 4.0.

TestDEN - creates personalized study guides for TOEFL (Teaching of English as a Foreign Language) students.

There are a number of features in this site that will appeal to students and teachers. One of the most important is the focus on content by combining traditional methods with interactive ones. Content is presented with both the teacher and student in mind. Student lessons are presented in a very appealing format with graphics used sparingly yet very effectively.

An added feature of this site is the use of computerized online unit multiple choice tests to evaluate student learning of the material. Once completed, the tests are submitted to the ACTDEN computer to be marked. A record is kept of all activity for students through a password system. These quiz tests are aimed at students in grades 7-12.

Log into the ACTDEN and see how online curriculum can supplement your own.

AskEric
(Educational Resources Information Center)
http://ericir.syr.edu

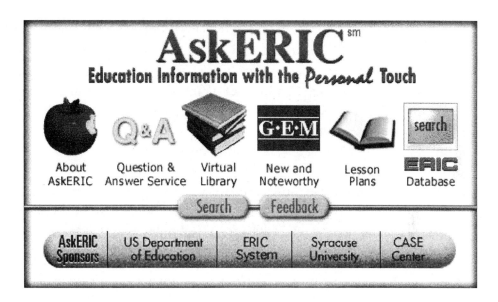

The AskEric website belongs to the Educational Resources Information Center (ERIC) and run by ACCESS ERIC which is sponsored by the U.S. Department of Education, Office of Educational Research and Improvement and administered by the National Library of Education. The ACCESS ERIC site contains the largest education database in the world, with over one million abstracts of documents and journal articles. The place for educational research.

The AskEric site was the first registered education site on the World Wide Web. The Virtual Library link contains more than 1,100 lesson plans, more than 20 listserv archives, 250 AskERIC InfoGuides and the AskERIC Toolbox. There are three main components of this site.

The first for educators and parents is the AskERIC question-answering service. This service is available 24 hours, 7 days a week with a 48 hour response time to answer questions about education.

The second component is the ERIC database This is the world's largest source of education information, containing more than one million abstracts of documents and journal articles on education research and practice. The database is updated monthly, ensuring timely and accurate information.

 The third component is the education listserv archive to over 20 educational listservs. A listserv is a mailing list which is targeted to a specific audience.

Some are very technical, others are general. Some are moderated, others unmoderated. Some are very active with over fifty messages a day, others have only a few messages a week. When you subscribe to a list, your name and e-mail is added to the list. You also usually receive a standard welcome letter introducing you to the list and any special instructions unique to the list. From that moment, any e-mail posted to the list by members will be sent to you. You can then read the discussions, send e-mail to individuals on the list or respond to the entire list. This link offers the educator a potpourri of some of the best listservs on the Internet. You don't have to join a particular list to be able to read the messages. Instead, you can browse through the archives available for each one. The beauty of the this AskERIC link to the listserv archives is the incredible time saving feature of the search function. All you have to do is select the listservs you want to search, describe what you are looking for, submit it and voila, specific information ready for you in an instant. Sure beats the old card catalog! Topics on these listservs range from charter schools, early childhood education, and educational technology to middle level education reading, projects, and vocational education. Current listserv archives include the following:

BigSix: Big Six approach to information literacy
http://askeric.org/Virtual/Listserv_Archives/Big6.html

Ecenet-L: Early Childhood Education/young children   (ages 0-8)
http://ericps.crc.uiuc.edu/eece/listserv.html

Edtech: Uses of technology in education for universities and school districts
http://askeric.org/Virtual/Listserv_Archives/EDTECH.html

K12Admin: K-12 School Administrators
http://ericir.syr.edu/Virtual/Listserv_Archives/k12admin-list.html

LM_NET: (Library Media Networking): serving the world- wide school library media community
http://ericir.syr.edu/lm_net/
(This list, co-founded by Michael Eisenberg and Peter Milbury is one of the best librarian mailing lists on the Internet. Every librarian should join this list!)

Middle-L: Middle level education
http://askeric.org/Virtual/Listserv_Archives/MIDDLE-L.html

Projects-L: Project Approach Listserv
http://ericps.crc.uiuc.edu/eece/listserv.html

Canada's SchoolNet
http://www.schoolnet.ca

Canada's SchoolNet is packed with information on Canada as well as information for a world wide audience interested in education. This searchable site has three main categories: SN Today, Learning Resources and Connect and over 20 Program topics on the side panel.

SN Today contains News, Cool Sites, Press Releases, Archives and the SchoolNet Magazine in PDF format. The Learning Resources section presents curriculum and education support materials. There are over 1,000 learning resources here under three categories: Curriculum Areas, General Interest and Federal and Related Institutions. The Curriculum Area contains a wealth of information on the following curriculum subjects: Adult Education, Art, Business Education, Career and Vocational Education, Computer and Information Technology, Entrepreneurship Studies, Family Studies, Health and Wellness, Integrated Subjects and Other, Language Arts, Mathematics, Physical Education, Sciences, Social Sciences, Social Studies and Special Needs Education. Under the Connect category can be found a hyperlist of schools on-line and the best Canadian school sites on the Web and advice for school website builders.

A unique and valuable source of information can be found under the Programs category. There are links to community programs, youth employment services, computers for schools, the SchoolNet News Network program for student journalists, information on First Nations, digital resources on Canadian history and culture. Be sure to check out the Virtual Products section to see the fantastic programs that have been developed for education.

Classroom Connect
http://www.classroom.com/

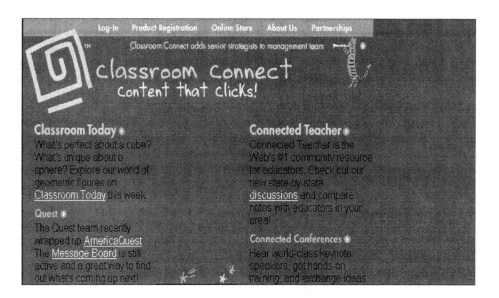

From humble beginnings at a kitchen table in Pennsylvania, this site is the web companion to scribbled notes on a piece of paper that eventually became the Classroom Connect Newsletter.

Classroom Today and the Connected Teacher are two of the main areas of this site. Classroom Today provides Internet links to the curriculum through student activities such as Daily and Weekly Questions, Kids' Quiz, Mystery Media, Survey Says, Connections and other activities. A Topics section provides topics to match curriculum. An Email Newsletter lets you find out more about Classroom Today topics each month. There is also a Teachers' Lounge with planning tools, a teaching guide and tips and ideas on measuring student progress.

The Connected Teacher section of the website links teachers to the latest in state-by-state discussions on education as well as keeping teachers informed on the latest ideas from fellow educators and world class keynoters at Connected Classroom Conferences. There is also an opportunity to read the presenters' handouts and participate in discussions from past conferences. An invaluable addition to any teacher's professional development is the Connected University. There is a free 30 day trial subscription. The following are some of the courses offered: Getting Started On The Internet, My First Web Page, The One Computer Classroom by Tom Snyder Productions, Reading and Language Arts Online, Science and Technology: A Natural Partnership, Teaching To Standards, A Technology Coordinator's Tool Kit, Using The Net To Create Thematic Units.

The once scribbled notes at the kitchen table have journeyed far and wide.

Community Learning Network

http://www.cln.org/

[What's New/CLN Update] [Network Nuggets] [Theme Page Index] [Alphabetical Index] [Navigation Map] [Search Engine]

Welcome to the Community Learning Network WWW home page. CLN is designed to help K-12 teachers integrate technology into their classrooms. We have over 265 menu pages with more than 5,800 annotated links to free resources on educational WWW sites -- all organized within an intuitive structure. Since September of 1996, visitors from 165 different countries have made over 16 million hits on the CLN Web site. Thank you and please come again!

The main menu of the Community Learning Network is a well organized source of educational resources for the K-12 teacher. The following links: Educational WWW Resources for K-12 Students and Teachers, Integrate the Internet into the Classroom, Learn More about the Internet, Professional Development in Information Technology and Province of British Columbia's K-12 Educational Community are followed by detailed descriptions and key words. True to its description "CLN provides direct links to exemplary educational WWW resources from our intuitive menus. By finding, previewing, describing, and linking to exemplary sites, CLN's staff save teachers an enormous amount of time that they would have wasted otherwise in fruitless browsing."

The CLN staff also review and update links to resources to eliminate the frustrations of searching for busy educators. Two valuable resources are the daily Network Nuggets and the CLN Update listservs which keep members informed to the latest Internet resources and updates on all the sites that have been added to the CLN site in the past week.

A very useful and fruitful resource for teachers are the CLN theme pages. Here can be found links which focus on a theme found in the K-12 curriculum. The curricular links provide informational resources for those interested in learning more about the topic while the instructional materials links provide support (e.g., lesson plans, instructional tips) for teachers.

The CLN staff have certainly made their site easy to use for the busy educator.

The Copernicus Education Gateway
http://edgate.com

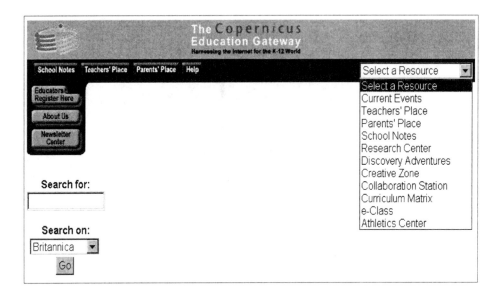

Click on the handy drop down Education Resources menu and quickly go to Current Events, Teachers' Place, Parents' Place, School Notes, Research Center, Discovery Adventures, Creative Zone, Collaboration Station, Curriculum Matrix, e-Class or the Athletics Center. If you need to look up a keyword or subject not found in the Education Resources menu, use the handy search engine. The search engine allows you to search the Copernicus site, the Encyclopedia Britannica and the Internet.

One key feature found here for teachers is the Curriculum Matrix. This very useful feature allows teachers to choose a subject: Science, Mathematics, Arts & Music, Health & Fitness, History, Communication, Reading, Civics, Economics, Geography and Writing and specify a grade from K-12. Clicking on Go takes you to an area of online learning resources, lesson plans and activities all linked to essential academic standards. This is a great starting point for any teacher doing unit and lesson planning. This feature also allows teachers to share their lesson plans and resources with other teachers.

If you need more resources for your lesson planning, head over to the Teachers' Place link and read about more curriculum ideas, lesson plans, professional development, grant information, special education and gifted programs. For something different and creative, click on the Creative Zone. You and your students will certainly enjoy the many wonderful and creative ideas available from the world's best Art museums, Creative Writing, Dance, Music, Theater and Filmaking sites. This is one site that should be bookmarked and visited often.

DiscoverySchool.com
http://www.discoveryschool.com/

As web companion to the very popular television show Discovery Channel , this website lives up to its slogan "The Thrill of Discovery in Your Classroom!" Resources for grades K-12 are easily available through a search engine which covers major subjects in the curriculum. Eight categories of links offer resources to make classroom teaching easier and fun.

The link to the Puzzlemaker category is by far my favorite destination. This wonderful tool has saved me and many teachers hours of work. It's fun, easy to use and the puzzles are a hit with students. There are word searches, word searches with hidden messages, computer generated mazes, criss-cross puzzles, number blocks, math squares, cryptograms, letter tiles and more!

The On TV category features TV calendars for The Learning Channel Elementary School programs for grades K-6 and the Discovery Program Assignment Discovery programs for grades 7-12. There is additional information on the TV shows and links to lesson plans. Another link gives information to teachers on upcoming prime time shows on Discovery Networks.

The Lesson Plans category contains lesson plans for grades K-12. You can see all the lesson plans on one page or just lessons for grades K-6 or 7-12.

Another great resource found here is Kathy Schrock's Guide for Educators. This well organized site is useful for enhancing curriculum and professional growth. It is updated daily to include the best sites for teaching and learning. There are more than 2,000 web links here!

Education World
http://www.education-world.com/

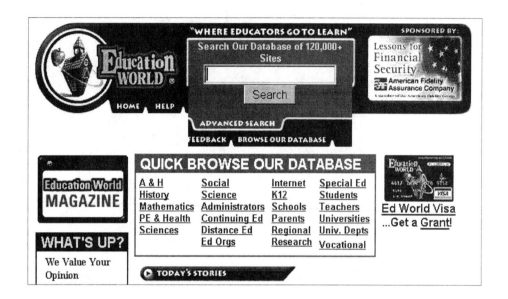

The site "where educators go to learn" boasts a searchable database of over 120,000+ sites! This well laid out site also offers timely information organized into the following topics and subtopics:

Original Content: WHAT'S NEW? Archives, Administrators, Books in Education, Curriculum, Great Sites, Lesson Planning, School Issues, Site Reviews, Special Themes, Teacher Lessons and Tech In Classroom.

Subject Centers: The Arts, Foreign Language, History, Language/Literature, Math, Physical Education/Health, Science, Social Sciences and Technology.

Communities: Counseling, Early Childhood Education, Higher Education, Parents, Preservice Education, Projects, Special Education, Students, Vocational Education.

Feature Areas: Best Of Series, Cool Schools, Education Standards, Employment Listings, Events Calendar, Grants Center, Holidays Center, Message Boards, News For Schools, Professional Development, Research Center, World Resources, World School Directory.

Support: FAQ (Frequently Asked Questions), About Us, Contact Us, Add A Site, Site Guide, Join Mailing Lists.

This site, whose motto "where educators go to learn" is a well deserved one.

Eduscapes
http://eduscapes.com/

A great starting point for any teacher beginning their unit and lesson planning is the 42explore link on this website. This is a marvelous collection of topics for K-12 students. Each week new topics are posted and previous topics are listed alphabetically and according to the date it was posted.

What I particularly like about the 42explore link is the authors' understanding of the nature of the Internet, the needs of teachers and students. The "four" in the title rhymes with "explore". The four also stands for four websites on a particular topic, because sometimes websites go down, content changes or it's just too slow. With four sites for teachers and students to access, chances are the information and resources will be available. There's nothing more frustrating to teachers and students when the key website for your topic and project isn't available anymore! With four to explore, the learning experiences for teachers and students will be a positive one.

This site also offers the Lamb's Technology Integration section. This invaluable section provides resources for parents, teachers, library/media specialists, administrators, and technology coordinators. Here can be found materials for workshops or for teacher's own professional development.

Highly recommended are the following two links: Lamb's Cool Starting Points for Teachers, Parents and Children and Seven Simple Starters: Realistic Internet Integration. The following seven questions are asked and answered: "What can I do daily or weekly? How can I connect to each subject area? What project would help me reach outside my classroom? How can I promote learning through technology? How can technology help students solve problems? How can my students share their projects with others? How can we use technology to create smiles?"

Head over to this site to find the answers to the above questions!

Enchanted Learning
http://www.EnchantedLearning.com/

This site has plenty to offer primary and elementary teachers (gr. Pre-K-6). Click on the link to Nursery Rhymes: Online Coloring Pages and find 25 well known nursery rhymes with pictures that you can color online, read and print out. There's even information on teaching rhymes to pre-readers, incorporating rhymes into other lessons, a nursery rhyme scavenger hunt and instructions on how to make a Nursery Rhyme Coloring Book.

Head over to Zoom Dinosaurs, a comprehensive online hypertext book about dinosaurs. It is designed for students of varying ages and levels of comprehension. There are over 60 printouts of dinosaurs for cut-outs used in dinosaur crafts, for coloring, for stencils and other uses. There's also information available on making a dinosaur book and online resources for grades K-2 and grades 3-4. In keeping with the dinosaur theme, there is also a dinosaur game, jokes and quizzes and links to museums, movies, stories, Art and stamps.

The resources don't stop with the extinction of the dinosaurs! It continues with a picture dictionary (in a number of different languages) with links to over 1,000 educational activities and games, and quizzes for pre-readers and students in grades 2-3. Wonderful resources are here for the clicking: astronomy, plants, Geography, explorers, inventors, rainforests, dinosaurs, sharks, whales, mammals, birds, butterflies, and many other animals.

There are hundreds of printouts, online information pages, coloring pages, illustrated glossaries, question-and-answer pages, and interactive puzzles here. You and your students will find plenty to do here and have fun learning it too.

ePALS Classroom Exchange
http://www.epals.com/

This remarkable, resource filled site is designed with the goal of making the Internet a positive and safe experience for busy classroom teachers and their students.   ePALS Classroom Exchange is the world's largest online K-12 classroom network, connecting more than 27,000 self registered classrooms with more than 1.7 million students in 130 countries around the world. Online since 1996, ePALS is currently available in English, French, Spanish, and German.

The main purpose of ePALS is to encourage teacher and student participation with other teachers and students anywhere in the world. Here's a fantastic and easy way to integrate the technology into the classroom and help students learn world history, geography, culture, another language and other facts about their global neighbors or neighbors from their own country or continent. Best of all the tools to make all this easy and possible are here at this website. In just a couple of minutes teachers can register their classrooms. A free ePALS membership comes with access to features such as e-mail, chat rooms, electronic greeting cards, instant messaging, newsletters, class websites and discussion boards.

There is an option here of providing students with a Teacher/Parent Monitored E-mail account. With Monitored E-mail, an adult creates an e-mail account for the child or student, and then can preview and approve every message sent to or from the child before it reaches its recipient. Aided by sophisticated filtering tools, the Monitor can quickly preview messages for inappropriate content before they are delivered to their recipient. If a message is questionable, it can be held or deleted instantly. The person who is monitoring the account has total discretion over how tightly to control the account. This is one option for parents and teachers to ensure a safe Internet experience for their children and students.

Check out other tools such as Instant Translation, World Maps and International Weather and teacher resources such as Interactive Projects, Online Resources, Manage Classroom Profiles, and 20th Century Retrospective. Once you log into ePALS, you'll quickly realize why this site is the world's largest online collaborative classroom network.

ePlay
http://eplay.com/

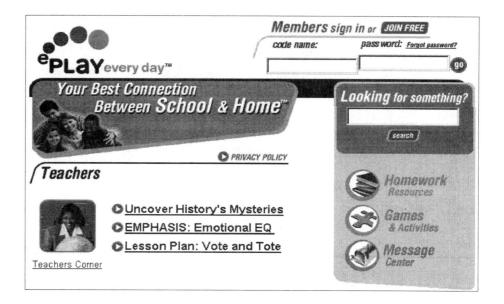

ePlay is a unique site on the Internet. Here's a site that does a marvelous job catering to three groups of people: teachers, parents and kids. It's a free educational site that has teaching resources, parenting help and homework tips, games, activities and more.

When you join ePlay as a teacher, you can create your own web page, register your classes, post homework assignments, update class notes and set up class Web links.

When you join ePlay as a parent, you can create your own parent's web page and connect to your child's home page where you can monitor your child's web links and access homework assignment.

Students too can create their own web page and even save their game scores as well as accessing their homework assignments on it. There is a built in safety feature for parents and teachers. Parents can review and edit sites saved by their children and teachers can set only those sites they want their class to access.

Wonderful lesson plans here for grades 3-5 Language Arts, Math, Geography, History and Science. If students click "online" they'll be able to work out the answers to the questions on screen. If they click "interactive" they'll be able to write the answer on the computer and then get feedback to see how they're doing. Finally, if they click print, they can print out the lessons.

ePlay is definitely worth a visit for teachers, parents and kids.

Headbone

http://www.headbone.com/

Headbone achieves the almost impossible task of appealing to both teachers and students (ages 8 to 14) by offering a safe, fun and structured way of exploring the Internet and practicing online research.

One activity which appeals to both teachers and students is The Headbone Derby. The Headbone Derby is a series of online adventures exploring themes and subjects such as Social Studies, Government, Science, History, Citizenship, Ecology and Inventions in Technology. Through this activity, students learn how to use search engines, how to critically evaluate online information, apply their knowledge of Geography, Geology, History, Government, Ecology, learn more about important subjects and apply problem solving and critical thinking skills. Teachers are given an online teachers guide which includes: grade specific preparation and planning sections, an outline of specific learning objectives, episode plot summaries, discussion topics and ideas for classroom activities to get the most out of the Headbone Derby series; an "Internet Primer" which provides reference materials on the basics of Web searching and guidance in using the Internet safely and a Frequently Asked Questions (FAQ) section which answers any questions you may have. It's easy to use and best of all, it's free!

Other activities in this versatile and educational site are Headbone Zone activities which include "Rags to Riches," an economic simulation game, "The Price of Fame," a buy, sell and trade celebrity stock game "Mars or Bust," a survival game "Fleet Kids,"a game that encourages learning through inquiry and getting kids started on the path to money smarts. There is also a 100% monitored Headbone Chat area for kids with chat games open according to a strict time schedule and limited to a set number of kids allowed entry into the chat rooms. (Parental permission needed for this feature for any child under 13.) There are eight chat rooms in all-two kids rooms, three teen rooms, a game room, a role-playing room and a room devoted to discussions and negotiations involving the Price of Fame game. This site is educational and fun.

Kentucky Migrant Technology Project
http://www.migrant.org/

Here's an innovative and constructive use of computer technology to overcome the challenge facing the migrant population i.e. low academic achievement among highly mobile migrant students and the lack of continuity of education among these students moving from one location to another. This site does not restrict itself to migrant students. In keeping with the original philosophy of sharing and caring on the Internet, the courses are free to use and available to all students, parents and teachers. The detailed and useful resources here (some courses are over 200 pages long!) cover subject matter across the core curriculum areas of Math, English, Science, Social Studies, Arts and Humanities, and Practical Living in grades 6-12. Uses of these online courses include: direct online learning for students, for enrichment or remediation, curriculum supplements for in-class and after-school programs, alternative school curriculum, and models to help teachers prepare for classes they teach.

The courses have been designed by practicing professional educators who have gone through a rigorous selection process. The courses are organized similarly to a regular school course, taught with daily lesson and activities followed by online quizzes and exams. The curriculum is correlated with ten sets of state core content standards or academic expectations, including Kentucky's Learning Goals and Academic Expectations. It also correlates with two nationally standardized tests, along with the GED test specifications and the Adult Basic Learning Exam. The Mathematics program was developed with the use of the NCTM Standards. In addition, all the resources needed to take the courses are found online as well. A few of the tasks may require access of some material at a local school library but these are very minimal.

This is a must site for anyone who wants to help students who have fallen "through the cracks" or needs help in education.

Learning Page.com
http://www.learningpage.com/

Are you a teacher or parent of preschool, kindergarten, first or second grade students? Do you need worksheets, lesson plans or tips? Then this site is for you. (There are worksheets here that can be used for the older grades as well.)

Click on the enter icon and find links to Basic Sheets, Theme Sheets, Tech Info and information on books. All of the lesson files and sheets are available as Adobe PDFs (Portable Document Format). All are downloadable and printable and free. You must have an Acrobat Reader to view the lessons. (The reader is free and available from **http://www.adobe.com/prodindex/acrobat/ readstep.html**). Once you have the Acrobat reader, simply click on the lessons you want and the lesson will appear in a new browser window. Further information is available by clicking on the Tech Info link.

The Basic Sheets category contains Zane-Blosner, D'Nealian and cursive alphabet sheets, with each sheet illustrating one alphabet letter with two words that start with that letter; Money sheets for recognizing, counting and coomparing pennies, nickels, dimes and quarters; Number sheets in Zane-Blosner, D'Nealian and American Sign Language formats.

The Theme category contains fact files, mural sheets, cutouts and teaching notes on oceans, zoo animals, dinosaurs, and insects/spiders; fun sheets on Pre-school to grade 2 Math, Language and Science subjects; and recommended reading for each of these themes.

This site adds new worksheets every week. A great site for instant help.

Lightspan.com
http://www.lightspan.com/

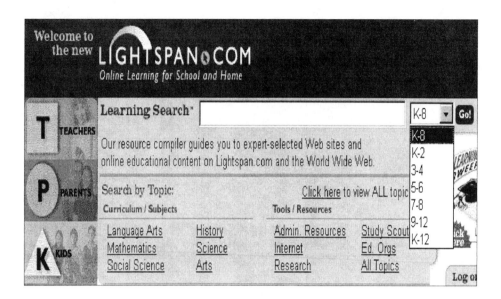

This site can rightly claim to have some of the best collaborative online projects, tools and resources for teachers on the Internet. Click on From the Teacher's Desk (K-2, 3-4, 5-6, 7-8) link and read about collaborative student projects, online field trips, expeditions, and more. My favorite areas here are the International Schools CyberFair where students worldwide work with their community in an international online competition; GeoGame where students learn about the geography and cultural diversity of our world in an exciting and unique way; Newsday which transforms students into reporters, editors, and graphic artists as they create their own newspaper based on articles submitted by student reporters from around the world. Also found here is the Project Registry which lists the best collaborative projects from around the world, searchable by topic, grade, or month. This registry allows teachers to do long term planning.

Another great area to explore for the busy educator is the For Your Classroom link. Here you'll find Award Maker a teacher tool that prints customized certificates for your students; Flashcards another tool that lets you create interactive flashcards in an instant. There are also more than 1,500 of the best online lesson plans and other learning activities for you and your students.

Other links include special Web Picks by noted educators Al Rogers and Yvonne Marie Andres, a Newsletter Sign-up, Online Safety Guidelines with suggestions for safe Internet surfing, Professional Development articles and technology links and commentary. Also, read about current issues in education policy by education and technology expert Andy Carvin. Don't miss this site.

Pacific Bell Knowledge Network Explorer
http://www.kn.pacbell.com/

The people at Pacific Bell started The Knowledge Network as a response to the needs of California's teachers, librarians, and students. Faced with a daunting array of technologies and the overwhelming need to train students and staff in the use of technology, the Knowledge Network developed new services for schools, libraries, and community colleges. Although The Knowledge Network was first conceived as a response to the needs of California, its many resources are available to everyone around the world via the Internet.

The Online Learning Guided Tour link offers resources for newcomers to the Internet, people who know their way around the Internet and for trainers and mentors. A popular site for newcomers and trainers alike is Blue Web'n. This is a library of sites for educators and librarians, sorted by subject, format and Dewey classification codes. You can also subscribe to the Blue Web'n Updates listserv and receive a weekly e-mail highlighting the Hot Sites of the Week plus 4 or 5 new Blue Web'n sites.

Another great tool for educators is Filamentality. Filamentality is a fill-in-the-blank interactive website that guides you through picking a topic, searching the Web, gathering good Internet sites, and turning Web resources into learning activities. To find out more, just click on the Filamentality link for more information and examples. Two other must see sites here for educators are the Web-based Lessons, Activities and More and the WebQuests links.

The Knowledge Network succeeds in its task to make technology and training less daunting for teachers, librarians and students.

PBS TeacherSource
http://www.pbs.org/teacherource/

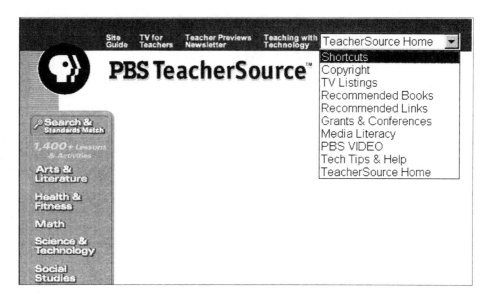

PBS (Public Broadcasting Service) is a private, non-profit media enterprise owned and operated by 348 public television stations in the United States. The PBS TeacherSource website is the web extension of PBS designed for Pre-K-12 educators.   Here can be found extensive curricular materials correlated to national and state standards, in-depth professional development services like Mathline and Scienceline and local community outreach services provided by public television stations across America.

A great starting place for all teachers is the Search & Standards Match tool. This tool is a great help for teachers in their search for relevant materials for their classrooms. It helps teachers to quickly and easily find materials by organizing resources into five main subject areas (Arts & Literature, Health & Fitness, Math, Science & Technology and Social Studies), searchable by subject, grade level, (Pre-Kindergarten to Post Secondary) keyword and correlated to more than 90 sets of national and state curriculum standards.   There is also the option of browsing the complete inventory of lessons gathered by subject.

The Teaching With Technology section contains invaluable tutorials for help on common computer applications and ideas for web-based lessons and suggestions for integrating technology into the curriculum.

Rounding out this website is the PBS Teacher Previews, a weekly online newsletter designed specifically for Pre-K-12 teachers. It's a great way to keep in touch with new Web features and details on PBS broadcast programs with educational taping rights, station resources and professional development.

Quia

http://www.quia.com/

categories		getting started
Astronomy (5 activities)	**Activity Manager** create your own games quizzes home pages	*How do I play games?*
Biology (15 activities)		*How do I create games and quizzes?*
Chemistry (13 activities)		
Chinese (3 activities)		*How do I make my own home page?*
English (15 activities)	**Quia! Directory** explore thousands of activities in over 40 subject areas	
French (219 activities)		*How do I use quiz sessions?*
Geography (51 activities)		
German (73 activities)	✹ **Log In**	*What does Quia mean?*
History (29 activities)		
Languages (596 activities)	✹ **New Users** free registration	*More...*
Latin (30 activities)	✹ **Top 50** most popular activities	**top activities**
Mathematics (33 activities)		*To / Two / Too*
Medicine (35 activities)	✹ **Quiz Sessions** student log in	*Music Mania*

Create your own worldwide classroom using sophisitcated yet easy-to-use technology. Quia, (pronounced key-uh) lets teachers do all this and more. Use Quia's free tools to create your own Internet-based educational activities like online flashcards, quizzes, matching games, word search puzzles, hangman games, and TV-game-show-style trivia games. Best of all, these activities can all be customized with the teacher's own content. So far, teachers have created over 250,000 activities on Quia, in subjects ranging from English, Spanish, Science, and Math, to Economics, Medicine, and World History.

The best activities are featured in the Quia Directory. In Spanish alone, there are several hundred activities to choose from, many of which are correlated to popular textbooks. It's easy to see why students love Quia--they are able to learn by playing educational games created just for them by their teachers. Quia also helps teachers teach better. Teachers can create their own class Web pages with messages to students and parents, links to favorite Web resources, and links to Quia activities that they have created. Teachers can also give quizzes online, and track and analyze student scores. Quia offers various reporting tools that allow educators to quickly access much more detailed information about student performance than they ever could by using pen-and-paper quizzes. And Quia couldn't be easier to use. Creating quizzes, games, and class webpages is free, only takes a few minutes, and there are plenty of instructions and samples to guide you along. This sure is different from making dittos on the ditto machine!

Room 108
http:// www.netrover.com/~kingskid/108.html

Room 108 is a website from primary teacher John Rickey with the Trillium Lakelands Board of Education in Ontario, Canada. It is a primary learning site that makes learning fun through educational games. There are animated picture books, games, Spelling, Math, Music and Art activities on this site.

The stories section contains unique and complete interactive picture books. Student interest is maintained using animated pictures, changing background music and sound effects. Students can sometimes click buttons to hear sounds that relate to the story. Most stories finish with a self marking comprehension test, that scores the student on errors. There are also interactive jigsaw and crossword puzzles and colouring activities based on the stories.

Enter the music section and music automatically comes on when entering a song page. Animations reflect the words of the song. Teachers can get the music for some songs which will have the guitar, lyrics and piano scored. Students can compose or change music and have it played back. Anyone playing the flute or piano will love this section-music is displayed on the screen and you can print out a copy of the music and play along. Visitors that don't own an instrument can have their computer keyboard turn into a drum set or an organ so they can play along with music also. There are almost 200 different compositions in different styles of music in the Jukebox section.

The Minute Math in the Math activities allows the teacher or student to customize a group of questions. This activity then marks the student's work.

Room 108 is a fun place to learn for all elementary students. Keep posted to this site for exciting upcoming additions and activities.

SCR*TEC

http://www.scrtec.org/

The South Central Regional Technology Education Consortium (SCR*TEC) representing Kansas, Missouri, Nebraska, Oklahoma and Texas, was formed to help teachers and other educators create, share, or find solutions to problems they encounter when integrating technology into education. With a region covering 6 million students and 400,000 teachers, SCR*TEC offers a tremendous network of experts.

Under the title of Network Solutions, there are links to such areas as: Planet Innovation, an area that has tools to assist school administrators and teachers in successfully planning, implementing, and evaluating technology; Profiler, an online collaboration tool strengthen your school district's ability to share expertise; Trackstar, an online interface to organize online resources and file them in a Trackstar database; www.4kids.org, a kid safe spot where a weekly newspaper feature searches three of four fun and educational sites giving kids the opportunity to be a 4Kids Detective of the week; www4teachers an indexed collection of online resources made by teachers for teachers such as making a quiz, web worksheet, a project based learning checklist or a trackstar; and Edlines, an educational web based newsletter features new SCR*TEC events, SCR*TEC resources, school pages, national educational technology news, Tech Tips, and a URL with suggestions for use in the classroom.

By far one of the most innovative and useful features of this website which makes it stand out from all the rest is the TracksStar feature. TrackStar is a program that allows teachers to organize a collection of websites into an interactive online presentation. It's an Internet web-based lesson plan maker. All lessons are searchable by keyword, subject and grade, themes and standards. You'll find some great ideas here, plus a lot of opportunities to create and share some great lesson plans for other teachers in the Internet community.

Tapped In
http://www.tappedin.org/

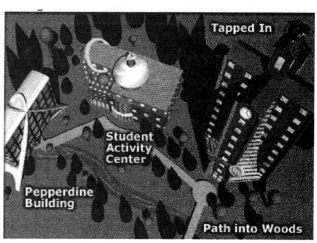

An aerial view of the TAPPED IN campus

TAPPED IN is a Teacher Professional Development Institute which goes a long way in helping teachers find the time to participate in high-quality professional development activities. It's also a way of maintaining support for teachers after an institute or workshop and encouraging sustained interaction among participating teachers. This is a teacher community where teachers with diverse interests, skills, and backgrounds can meet and learn from one another; where teachers can be exposed to not one but many education reform concepts and approaches; where teachers from across the country and world can find high-quality resources in minutes rather than hours.

How is this all done? By MUVE (multi-user virtual environment) technology. Although the technology sounds daunting, it's really pretty amazing stuff. You don't have to be a techno wizard to use it. MUVE combines the convenience of a chat room with the versatility of a real life classroom you can talk in real time, use a whiteboard, project notes, and even share URLs (Universal Resource Locators) to everyone in the room to see. There is an extensive FAQ (Frequently Asked Questions) section and extensive Help Guides and Tips to help you get the most out of your TAPPED IN experience. With over 8,000 members made up of K-12 teachers, Staff Developers, Preservice Teachers, School Administrators, Education Researchers, Librarians and others, there's a good chance you'll learn something new and bring back a different perspective to your class and school.

Among the many organizations partnering with TAPPED IN and have their offices here are the following: The Math Forum, ICONnect (an initiative of the American Association of School Librarians), PALS (Performance Assessment Links in Science) , ED's Oasis, Kentucky Department of Education and others.

TeachersFirst

http://www.teachersfirst.com/

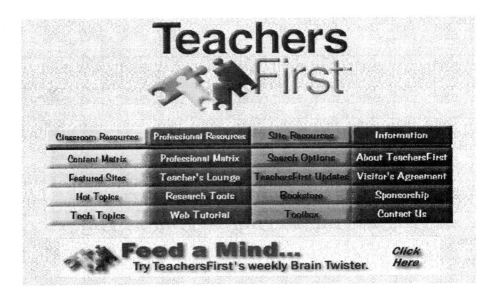

TeachersFirst is a website designed to meet the needs of K-12 "teachers in the trenches." It accomplishes this goal by focusing on practical resources that teachers need in the classroom. Each resource is selected and reviewed by one of TeachersFirst's reviewers, all of whom have classroom teaching experience. These reviewed resources are then grouped by subject and grade level, so that teachers can find what they need quickly.

The Content Matrix simplifies the finding of lesson materials and resources on the TeachersFirst website. Here resources and lessons can be searched by subject, or by keyword. Each TeachersFirst review provides a color-coded grade level for elementary, middle and high school. There is also a Professional Resources Matrix with resources available under the following three categories: Teaching Strategies, Special Education in the Classroom and Professional Development. This is a great place to find resources for new teachers.

A Learning the Web section offers simple tutorials and explanations of Internet services and terminology. A Toolbox section provides links to free downloads of browser enhancements that let you view and print documents, play sound or video files, or view 3D animations on your browser.

To keep up with the latest resources, click on Hot Topics and find current news or topical resources for the classroom or click on the Featured Sites section each week. If you prefer to have someone send you the latest information, subscribe to the TeachersFirst Updates e-mail monthly newsletter. If you're looking for practical classroom information, you'll find it here at the Teachers First website.

Teachers.Net

http://www.teachers.net/

The Ultimate Teacher's Resource!

chat center | chatboards | chatroom | meetings | mailrings | lessons | curricula | ref desk | jobs | advertise

RESOURCES

▶ NEW: GAZETTE NEW!
▶ K12 SUPPLIES
▶ CHAT CENTER
▶ LESSON PLANS
▶ CHATBOARDS
▶ LIVE CHATROOMS
▶ JOB CENTER
▶ 4 BLOCKS COLUMN
▶ LIVE MEETINGS
▶ MEETING ARCHIVE
▶ MAILRINGS
▶ POSTCARDS
▶ BOOKSHELF
▶ CURRICULUM
▶ CALENDAR
▶ LIBRARY
▶ WEB TOOLS
▶ WEBRING
▶ SEARCH
▶ ADD URL
▶ CATALOG
▶ ADVERTISE

Teachers.Net is a diverse family of Internet resources committed to providing free mentoring support to every segment of the education profession worldwide. "Family" is a particularly appropriate descriptor to apply in the case of this attractive and bustling niche on the World Wide Web. The Teachers.Net family includes Administrators.Net; Retired Teachers.Net; Australian Teachers.Net; Canadian Teachers.Net; California Teachers.Net and Texas Teachers.Net, with plans for continued growth into additional geographic and topical areas.

"Family" describes the atmosphere on dozens of Teachers.Net discussion boards which meet the needs of tens of thousands of educators and school administrators from every grade level, specialty, and curricular area.

Site "regulars" check in daily to respond to questions and pleas for help from colleagues they've never met. "Newbies" are welcomed and immediately caught up in the site's mission to provide peer support. Similar support is enjoyed by thousands on the e-mail discussion groups and in the chatrooms.

A busy schedule of live chats features guest experts on topics related to the interests and needs of today's educators. Special area and grade level meetings are peer moderated and most chat transcripts are archived. The Gazette e-zine is posted online monthly, featuring articles written by members of the Teachers.Net community and by well-known and respected experts from the world of Education, written exclusively for Teachers.Net.

Educators needing assistance with any topic, from web page building to classroom management, from literacy education to science fair projects, will find free and enthusiastic support at Teachers.Net. Join the family! I'm sure glad I did!

Top Parent Sites

Family.Com
http://family.go.com/

The Disney people have capitalized on their trusted name and have set up this very well organized and resource rich family site. Set up in a magazine type format with visually appealing graphics accompanying text on topical features, this site is geared for parents. Information is arranged under the following main categories: Activities, Food, Pets, Travel, Baby and Pregnancy, Health, Parenting and Learning.

Clicking on the Learning Category link will take you to an education page with the following topics and information: Education Bank, Homework Helper, Computing Corner, Homeschooling Center and Reading Room as well as a tip of the day, learning checklists, articles, schools in the news and a link to message boards.

Message boards are a great way to find information and to share tips and ideas with other parents. There are message boards here to cover parenting issues from the following categories: all about you, Pregnancy, Your Kids, Learning, Health, Family Ties, Home, Activities and Travel.

Even though this site is packed with information, there are search engines available to sort through information quickly and efficiently by using key word searches or by clicking on topics. On the Education page, the search engine allowed you to pick education topics and match it with your child's age. On the home page, the recipe finder can track down over 15,000 recipes. This is a handy tool when kids ask that never ending question "what's for dinner?"

FamilyEducation Network
http://familyeducation.com/

FamilyEducation.com is the award winning parenting website of the FamilyEducation Network found at **http://www.fen.com** This network includes the well known websites **schoolcash.com, funbrain.com, teachervision.com, myschoolonline.com**, and **infoplease.com** It is the largest K-12 Internet community for parents, teachers and students.

FamilyEducation.com is packed with information for parents and educators in the following eleven categories: Ages and Grades, Activities, News and Hot Topics, School Help, Parenting Challenges, Special Needs, Family Finance, Software Downloads, What Works, Expert Advice and Message Boards. Under each category are extensive subtopics. All the information on the website is searchable by keyword and age (Pre-School and Younger to High School and College Planning).

An innovative feature found here was today's poll. Here I was asked a question, but also given the opportunity to follow up the question with my own comments on a discussion board. If I didn't want to post a comment, I could read comments or click on links to find more information on the poll's topic. Now that's what I like about this site's use of the technology, providing an interactive environment and at the same time valuing my time, my interests and opinions. This one feature alone is well worth your time.

For parents (and teachers) wanting more information on helping children and students with school work, click on the School Help link. Topics here range from Homework Help, School Subjects, to Tests and Grades, From Our Experts, The Help Desk and Newsletter Signup. If you want to get help from a school counselor for a specific concern, there is one each for grades K-5, 6-8, 9-12 and beyond and Pre-K-12. Ask them a question and check back for their replies. If you want to keep up with specific grades and issues, there are monthly newsletters to help you out. Lots of choices here for all kinds of topics and issues in education. Well worth your time as a parent or teacher.

Parent Soup
http://www.parentsoup.com/

Parent Soup is part of the iVillage.com: The Women's Network. Here's a network of women helping each other to provide all kinds of solutions to all kinds of problems. iVillage.com does this through the use of interactive tools, resident experts, feature articles and a network of women members. It's a huge, well organized and well run network. Parent Soup is one of its channels.

The Parent Soup website or channel, is a very extensive offering of solutions to the challenges of parenting. Solutions can be found here from a team of experts, communities for specific stages of parenting, tools, interactive message boards, feature articles, newsletters, polls and links to shopping.

I headed to the education central link to see the solutions to education. I was not disappointed. Information here is warmly and lovingly presented by brightly colored icons that could have been drawn by your own children. Categories with titles such as Homeroom, Grades, Subjects, Vocabulary List and Passing Notes, convey the feel of being in a real school.

The Grades category, is divided into pre-school, elementary, junior/middle, and high school. Searching for information here is simplified by the use of an individualized search engine for each of these categories. You can quickly and easily zero in on your child's grade and in no time at all start reading about general aspects of the grade, developmental milestones, curriculum and how you can help. As a parent and teacher, I enjoyed reading and spending time on the grades I teach and on my own children's grades.

I highly recommend the iVillage.com network and the Parent Soup website for solutions to parenting and education challenges for you and your children.

Parenting Today's Teen
http://www.parentingteens.com/

Anyone who has a teenager, or who interacts with teens on a daily basis should visit this site. In a newsletter type format, feature articles on timely topics can be found in the center of the homepage surrounded by columns focusing on teenage issues.

Columns with titles such as: Ask The Expert, Book Reviews, Communication, Delinquency Prevention, Education, Humor, Life Skills, Living With Parents, Living With Teens, Online Issues, Single Parenting, Software Reviews, Speak Out, Special Needs, Spirituality and Step Families provide invaluable resources to deal with teens. There is also a link to an archive of past articles.

This site understands the difficulties parents, teachers and teens often have communicating with each other and the sometimes dangerous results and consequences when there is a lack of communication and understanding. To help with these difficulties and challenges, The Parent Forum and Chat features have been designed to offer suggestions and questions from other parents. An especially useful feature for busy parents is the Online Parenting Classes feature found here. Signup for a free parenting class without leaving your home.

Other helpful features include links to other parenting resources, a parenting support group listserv where parents of teens can come together and find support, encouragement and advice from other parents of teens via e-mail and a bookstore featuring books on parenting issues.

I found this site to be a very useful resource for parents and teachers who want to better understand their teenage children and students.

Surfing The Net With Kids
http://www.surfnetkids.com/

Barbara J. Feldman, the creator of Surfing The Net With Kids website has combined her skills and experience as a programmer, computer consultant, newsletter publisher, shareware author, mom and syndicated newspaper columnist to produce a first rate website for families and kids. Each week, Barbara writes site reviews for kids and families based on a theme.

Website reviews are listed here under the following categories: Arts, Crafts, Music, Computers and Web, Games, Hobbies, Geography, Holidays, History, Language Arts, Math, Parents and Teachers, Preschool and Kindergarten, Science. Reviews are also available by a keyword search or by a popup menu. Each theme has up to five site reviews based on a rating system of spectacular (five stars), wonderful, (four stars) and great (three stars). There is even an Honorable Mentions section listing links to new discoveries or sites that didn't make it into her newspaper column because of space constraints. There are also links to reader suggestions, toys, books and jokes all related to the theme.

Other features listed here are Calendar, Forum, Games and Newsletter. The Calendar lists important dates, major holidays and anniversaries. There are also links to educational website reviews and contests of interest to parents, teachers and students. It is updated weekly, and lists four weeks of events. The Forum is a discussion board moderated by Barbara to ask Internet questions and share ideas with other parents and teachers. Click on the Games link and choose Word, Math, Science, History and Holiday, Picture, Arcade, Trivia, Art and Music games. A free semi-weekly newsletter keeps readers in touch with the best online sites for families and teachers.

This is a wonderful site for teachers and parents looking for carefully reviewed theme based and rated websites for their students and children.

Top Kid's Sites

ALFY

http://www.alfy.com/

ALFY is the largest web portal for kids. It is designed especially for 3-9 year olds to safely experience the resources of the Internet. This is also a great site for parents and teachers. Here you can find thematic units, lesson plans, lesson builders, brain teasers, homepage makers, award makers and great links to educational sites and more.

ALFY's entirely graphical interface is with colorful, animated graphics, and use of sounds, make this site incredibly easy for young kids to navigate - even pre-readers! There are hundreds of engaging activities designed to stimulate and captivate young minds.

The site is well organized into eight main areas: The Brain Train, Music Mania, Storyville, Create!, The Clubhouse, Surprises, ALFY's Arcade and ALFY's Cool Sites. Click on The Brain Train and have your child experience geometric figures, spatial relations, and time concepts. Music Mania has different musical instruments, a place for kids to record their melodies, and listen to their creations. Go to Storyville and have your child take part in interactive stories, and sign their own online masterpieces. Create! has opportunities for creative expression in the virtual art studio. The Surprise area features new jokes and riddles, and a chance to visit their own adopted pet and watch it grow. A wonderful site for the entire family!

Amazing Kids
http://www.amazing-kids.org/

Celebrating the Achievements of Children™

Amazing Kids is a site designed to inspire excellence in children. This is accomplished through the following programs: Amazing Kids! of the Month, Amazing Mentors Program, Amazing Kids! Webspace (contains a virtual library for writers and a virtual art gallery for artists), Amazing Kids Television Program, Amazing Kids Contests and Amazing Kids Scholarship Fund. If you know an Amazing Kid, surf over to this site and check it out.

Berit's Best Sites for Children
http://www.beritsbest.com

Librarian Berit Erickson has searched far and wide to present the Web's best 1,000 sites for kids. There are categories for sites that are Just For Fun, sites for Holidays and Seasons, Creatures Great and Small, Serious Stuff, Kids on the Net and Safe Surfing. There is also a ranking of the Top 25 websites with rankings from previous weeks to the number of weeks they've been on her list.

The recommended sites here are geared to children up to the age of 12. Each site is rated for Content, Organization, Ease of Use, Appearance, Bells and Whistles, Audience, Credibility, Fees and Privacy. Only the best sites that meet these criteria are chosen for Berit's Best. And she is very picky!

Bonus.Com
http://bonus.com/

This site, billed as a SuperSite for Kids is a well designed, easy to follow website with activities ranging from the preschooler to the teenager, teacher and parent. The owners' commitment to appropriate content and kid friendly sites makes this website as safe as possible on an ever-changing Internet. In keeping with this philosophy, there is no two-way chat area. Every piece of content is hand-selected for a younger audience by the Bonus.com editors.

Bonus.com has over 2,000 activities that take participants from the ocean depths to the farthest reaches in space. There is so much to do at this site, that parents, teachers and especially kids will each find something to come back to over and over again. Set aside a couple of hours and have fun at Bonus.com.

CBC4Kids
http://www.cbc4kids.ca/

Students between the ages of 8 to 14, their parents and teachers will enjoy this site from the Canadian Broadcasting Corporation. Not only is it safe and entertaining, it's also educational. There are six main subject areas here: News and Sports (daily news and sports stories, quizzes), The Lab (weekly science news and quizzes), Words (word games, creative writing opportunities and book reviews), Music (Guess That Instrument and Name That Classical Tune), Time (a look back at history and forward to the future) and Kids Club (games and discussions, pets polls and more). Includes a teacher's guide too!

Cyberkids

http://www.cyberkids.com/

Budding student composers, writers and artists between the ages of 7 and 12 are invited to send their masterpieces here for publication. In addition to art and writing, this site also encourages students to send in material. They will publish student brain teasers, games, jokes, and multimedia creations.

Students also get the opportunity to do software, book, movie, video and electronic product reviews, interviews of celebrities in the movie and music industries.

Over at the Kids Connect area, kids can communicate with other kids in chat rooms and on message boards and discuss the latest reviews, news and their own views.

Cyberteens

http://www.cyberteens.com/

Cyberteens ... where creative teens rule

Cyberteens.com is the older sibling of the cyberkids.com website. Teens nineteen and under are encouraged to send stories, poems, editorials, art, photos, comics, music compositions, reviews of software, websites, books and Shockwave movies for publication.

Wonderful examples of teenage art, music, poetry, stories and Shockwave movies can be viewed here. Once the creations have been submitted, your teen can try out the many games or connect up with other teens in the chat areas.

FreeZone

http://www.freezone.com/

FreeZone is a huge online community for kids 8-14. Here's a place where kids can contribute their ideas for stories, books, movies, music reviews and build their own webpages. They can put their expertise and advice to good use as a FreeZone reporter, Jr. Chat Jockey, Advice Giver, member of the Sports Squad, Smarty Pants Team, Tech Know Team and Culture Crew in ten bulletin boards and scheduled chat rooms.

It's a fun and safe place for kids. The site is monitored and screened by trained adult employees and has been recognized for its high safety and privacy standards by Time, Newsweek, Family PC, and Oprah Winfrey. Adults monitor the Chat Box at all times, screen all bulletin board messages, screen all postcards, check all Home Page Constructor pages, files and check all BrainStorm KiDecision responses.

Funbrain.com

http://www.funbrain.com/

Funbrain.com is a great place to have fun for the brain. This site makes it very easy to search for all kinds of great games. You can search a game by name or by the following subjects: Math, Language Arts, Science, History, Music, Geography and Art and then click on your child's or student's grade and zero in on the right game to play.

Teachers will also find great tools here for their classrooms. A Quiz Lab lets you create your own quizzes, access thousands of quizzes designed by teachers world-wide, allow students to take quizzes over the Internet, in the classroom, in the library, or at home. The Quiz Lab will get quiz results for you automatically via e-mail and it even grades them for you.

This site will certainly give any kid's brain a fun workout (and an adult's too!)

Funschool.com
http://www.funschool.com/

Need activities for your pre-schooler to your sixth grader? This regularly updated site, uses Java applets to engage children in over 300 activities such as cartoon makers, map puzzles, number and letter matching, connecting the numbers, animal safaris, paint brush Math to more challenging games for older children. Go ahead and connect those dots.

Girl Tech
http://www.girltech.com/

Whoever thought that computers and the Internet were geared for boys, has never visited Girl Tech. Here's a site that's safe for girls between the ages of 12 and 18. A Girl Powered Search Engine helps girls search the Internet for their favorite sites without the danger of being exposed to inappropriate content. The chat area is known as Chick Chat (read the reasons behind the choice of this name—it'll surprise you). It's a place for girls to communicate, give and get advice, post messages to friends and express ideas. There's even a Boy Talk area to help bridge communication between the genders.

The Girls Galaxy area is a place for girls to dream and pursue their goals by featuring women of the past, present and future as role models. InventHer is another section that encourages girls to learn more about women inventors and think creatively. Other areas include a Game Café, Sports, Girl Views, Tech Trips and Bow-Tique.

KidsCom
http://www.kidscom.com/

Once on this site, it's easy to see why hundreds of thousands of kids between the ages of 4-15 have made it one of the longest running kid sites on the Internet.

Here's a safe site where kids get to chat, play games, write stories, take polls, find and write other kids for pen pals and get video game cheats and tips.

Start by clicking on any of the following categories: Around The World gives kids an opportunity to make their opinions heard by presidents and prime ministers; Make New Friends lets kids chat with other kids 11 and younger and in another chat wall, chat with kids 12 to 15; Kids Talk About has daily jokes, polls and story starters; Just For Fun has games, tips and tricks and Skeeter's Music Machine where you can make your own music; Cool Stuff gives kids a chance to earn KidsKash points.

Kids Domain
http://www.kidsdomain.com/

Looking for software for your kids or for yourself? Don't know where to go or who to trust? The Kid's Domain, run by a staff of parents is the place to find PC, Mac Shareware and Freeware Programs for kids which are recommended by families and teachers. Here you'll find demos, honest in-depth reviews, articles about children's software, programming for kids and free graphics. There are also contests, online games, crafts, free downloads, reviews, teaching tips, free graphics, and holiday pages with fun activities.

The staff of parents carefully select every item that goes on the site. The site is updated and expanded weekly, with 800+ commercial software reviews, 2000+ downloadable programs, 600+ online games, 2000+ icons, 750+ hand picked links-all for kids and families. A highly recommended site for kids and parents.

Squigly's Playhouse
http://www.SquiglysPlayhouse.com/

Squigly's Playhouse is a fun and safe place for kids to play on the internet. There are on-line games, cool craft ideas and coloring pictures, pencil puzzles, a writing corner, jokes and riddles, brain teasers, contest, desktop pictures, boredom busters, polls and more. Activities may be copied for use in the classroom and for home. Children's submissions are always welcome and the theme changes every 3-4 weeks.

Weekly Reader Galaxy
http://www.weeklyreader.com/

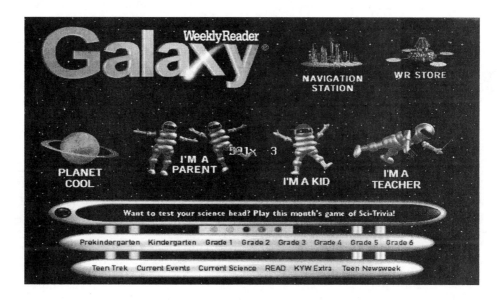

Weekly Reader Galaxy is a newspaper for kids website. It's designed to get kids from pre-kindergarten to grade 10 reading. There are a variety of activities on this site for each grade from pre-kindergarten to grade 6 and special sections for teens. Take a poll, check out the weekly news updates, try the science activities, enter some great contests and win cool prizes, go on a field trip with a kid correspondent. This is no ordinary online newspaper. There's a lot here of interest to any kid and any teacher.

Zeeks.Com

http://www.zeeks.com/

Zeeks.com is a free, safe, all-in-one Internet destination for kids ages 6–13. It's a place where kids can have fun, talk to other kids, do research, play games, surf the Web, and much more! There's a big emphasis on safety at Zeeks.com. Safety is maintained by free ZeekSafe filtering software. When this filtering software is downloaded on to your browser, it keeps children safe when they are off the Zeeks site. (ZeekSafe, blocks out more than 150,000 sites that contain content deemed unsuitable for children between the ages of 6–13. The ZeekSafe word filter also scans millions of pages for inappropriate content. These pages are also blocked while ZeekSafe is active. The list of blocked sites is updated often and updates are free of charge.) Safety is also maintained by having kids join as members of Club Zeeks to use certain features, such as Calendar, game reviews, and Factory. Parental permission is needed for children under 13 to use e-mail, chat, and ZeekStore. Chat rooms are strictly monitored, and monitors are trained to keep children from sharing personal information, discussing inappropriate topics, or verbally abusing other chatters. A "swear word" filter is also built into the chat program to snag bad words before they appear on the child's screen.

This is a site where kids can have fun and learn a lot at the same time. There are contests, Science facts, an Ask Margo area where kids can ask questions if they have a problem with school or friends or about anything at all. Andy's Tech Tips is a great place for techy questions. There's also a place to create a web project, send out Zeekcards, make up a personalized calendar and play over 180 games once all the school research is done for the day!

Chapter 2

Sites for Educational Standards, Lesson Plans and Themes

"Our progress as a nation can be no swifter than our progress in education. The human mind is our fundamental resource."

John F. Kennedy

Educational Standards

There are a number of very informative sites on the Internet that link state and provincial standards to curriculum outcomes by grades. These sites also allow teachers to find resources, lesson plans and assessment tools that tie into each grade level and outcome. Below I've listed some of the more popular sites.

Achieve.org
http://www.achieve.org/

Achieve's database serves as a national clearinghouse on state and international standards. It is a searchable database of 40 state and international academic standards in the following subjects: English, Mathematics, Science, and Social Studies. It is organized by subject, state, grade level, topic, and keyword.

Developing Educational Standards
http://PutnamValleySchools.org/Standards.html

Developing Educational Standards is a detailed, annotated list of Internet sites with K-12 educational standards and curriculum frameworks documents, maintained by Charles Hill and the Putnam Valley Schools in New York, USA.

Making Standards Matter 1999
http//www.aft.org/edissues/standards99/

Making Standards Matter is an annual report by the American Federation of Teachers. This very informative report analyzes the quality of the academic standards in the 50 states, the District of Columbia, and Puerto Rico. It also monitors the extent to which those standards are driving education reform. The report provides commentary on each state's standards, highlighting areas of strength and pinpointing weaknesses that must be addressed to improve the standards; states' activities and intentions to assess whether students are meeting the standards, whether states are providing extra academic help to students who are having difficulty meeting the standards, and whether states are attaching meaningful consequences to the standards so that students and others take them seriously.

The report provides a state by state analysis and responses by the states to the report. Some very interesting trends are highlighted over the years. I found the report very instructional to read confirming some of my own teaching experiences over the years. Check out how your own state is doing.

State Standards
http://www.education-world.com/standards/state/

If you need to find your state's education standard, this is the place. Searchable by subject and grade level. Includes links to the state's main page.

State Standards Coupled to Lesson Plans and Resources
http://www.statestandards.com/

Click on a state or choose a state from the drop down menu box. A description of the state standard for the subject and grade as well as up-to-date information on state standards appears. The innovative feature of this site is when you click on a subject standard. The description of the standard is automatically put in the keyword search box of the Microsoft Lesson Connection search engine which goes out to the Internet for a resource match. Highly recommended.

The ERIC Clearinghouse on Assessment and Evaluation
http://ericae.net/

This is a very popular and excellent site to find balanced information concerning educational assessment, evaluation and research methodology. There are over 350 searchable full text books and articles in the Assessment Library. An innovative feature found here is the recording of the number of times an article was read and the last time it was accessed. It gives you an idea of what is being widely read and discussed.

State and Provincial Standards
Illinois
Chicago Public Schools Instructional Intranet
http://intranet.cps.k12.il.us/

In Chicago, public school students are taught curriculum based on the Chicago Academic Standards (CAS) which are in turn based on the Illinois Learning Standards. This website contains the academic standards for grades K-12 for Language Arts, Mathematics, Social Studies and Science in HTML and PDF formats. A link for each grade accesses the state goals for that grade and subject as well as the corresponding Chicago Academic Standards (CAS), and Curriculum Framework Statements (CFS) for that goal. New Structured Curriculum Handbooks were developed to assist teachers in implementing standards-based curricula in the four core subject areas for which Chicago Public Schools has established standards. Detailed daily lesson plans for the structured curriculum can be found here and downloaded in PDF format. Links available to other teacher resources. I highly recommend a visit to this site.

Make the Link to Illinois Learning Standards
http://www.stclair.k12.il.us/makethelink/mlgrid.htm

The St. Clair County Regional Office of Education has designed a Standards Grid which links to sites that support the benchmarks from the Illinois Learning Standards. Resources for Language Arts, Math, Science, Social Studies, Health and Physical Education, Fine Arts and Foreign Languages in

Early Elementary, Late Elementary, Middle School, Early High School and Late High School can be found here.

Louisiana
Making Connections
http://www.lcet.doe.state.la.us/conn/

Louisiana's learning content standards, benchmarks and supporting resources can be found on this site. The standards cover Arts, English, Language Arts, Foreign Language, Math, Science, Social Studies, and Foundation Skills. Resources geared to the benchmarks and specific grades are searchable by resource type (lesson plans, website resources, software products, assessment items), title, keyword, grade (pre-K-12), strand, benchmark, software publisher, software platform and software type. Each lesson plan, website review and software preview submitted to the site are carefully reviewed to ensure that only the best is posted on the Making Connections site.

Maryland
Curriculum Internet Links
http://www.howard.k12.md.us/connections/

This resource was created by teachers of the Howard County Public School system in Maryland. Just click on a grade level from K-12 or on a subject area. There are great links here to wonderful Internet resources which can be used by all teachers. I found some great sites here for my own class.

Texas
Curriculum Connections Index
(K-8) http://www.tcet.unt.edu/START/connect.htm
(9-12) http://www.tcet.unt.edu/START/res_912.htm

This index contains connections between the Texas Essential Knowledge and Skills (TEKS) and Technology Applications. This is a very well thought out and complete site offering resources for K-8 in the subjects of Language Arts and Reading, Mathematics, Social Studies and Science as well as Curriculum Connections Planning Tools. High School subjects for grades 9-12 covered here include Computer Science, Desktop Publishing, Digital Graphic/ Animation, Multimedia Production, Video Technology, Web Mastering and

Independent Study in Technology Applications. Great project ideas and links to subject specific resources can also be found here.   A chart of an index of weblinks which categorizes resources by grade and subject can be found at:
http://www.tcet.unt.edu/START/wwwcode.htm
This site should definitely be visited and explored for its great resources.

Utah
UtahLink
http://www.uen.org/utahlink/
http://www.uen.org/cgi-bin/websql/lessons/curriculum.hts
(Searchable Curriculum Database)

Complete lesson plans with detailed objectives, standards, learning outcomes, material list, links to rubrics, sample activities and more can be found and accessed here. This site gives a number of options for viewing the materials. Click on the Site Map and choose from Core Curriculum Online to view course descriptions of all available courses; or click on the Query Lesson Plans link to access a searchable curriculum database for lesson plans. Whichever method you choose, you'll certainly be pleased with the results. A great site.

Canada: Ontario

Curriculum Resources
http://www.ocdsb.edu.on.ca/Teacher_Res/curriculum.htm

The Staff Room for Ontario's Teachers
http://www.odyssey.on.ca/~elaine.coxon/

Link to Learning
http://www.linktolearning.com/

These three sites are specifically geared for Internet resources by subject, grade and strand for the Ontario elementary curriculum. They are great places to start gathering resources for elementary teachers everywhere. Just click and visit these sites to find assessment and evaluation tools, rubrics, and report card comments that you'll be able to use in your school and classroom.

Curriculum Matrix
http://www.copernicus-matrix.com/

The Curriculum Matrix is a search engine that allows searching by academic standard, grade level and subject. Great online learning resources, lesson plans and activities all connected to academic standards can be accessed here.

ExplorAsource
http://www.explorasource.com/educator/

Find instructional resource materials cross-referenced to educational standards that meet the needs of your students or children. The educational resources referenced here include books, CDs, videos and websites. Included here are over 130 standards documents from around the country representing over 35 states and a growing number of districts. Try out the sample searches.

McREL (Mid-Continent Research for Education and Learning)
http://www.mcrel.org/

Click on the McRel Shortcuts link to the McRel Standards Database. Here you'll find standards and benchmarks for K-12 education. Browse or search the standards and benchmarks or click on activities linked to the standards and benchmarks. Check the Hotlinks by Subject area for more lesson plan ideas.

PBS TeacherSource
http://www.pbs.org/teachersource/

PBS TeacherSource correlates Language Arts, History, Math, and Social Studies lessons to more than 90 sets of national and state curriculum standards. Search for lesson plans by grade and subject, and find correlations to select national and state standards to more than 1,400 lessons and activities.

Lesson Plan Sites

AskERIC Lesson Plans
http://ericir.syr.edu/Virtual/Lessons/

The AskEric Lesson Plan Collection contains more than 1,100 lesson plans written by teachers. Browse the site by subject or search the entire collection.

The Academy Curriculum Exchange
http://ofcn.org/cyber.serv/academy/ace/

700 K-12 lesson plans originally from the Columbia Education Center's Summer Workshops are hosted here. They were created by classroom teachers for their own class and shared here. Lesson plans are organized by Elementary (K-5), Intermediate (6-8) and High School (9-12) for Language, Mathematics, Science, Social Studies and a Miscellaneous section. One click and you're on your way to some great ideas.

The Awesome Library K-12 Education Directory
http://www.awesomelibrary.org/

This is an "awesome" collection. Over 14,000 resources. Searchable.

Blue Web'n Learning Sites Library
http://kn.pacbell.com/wired/bluewebn/

Blue Ribbon learning sites are classified here by web based tutorials, activities, projects, unit and lesson plans, hotlists, other resources and references and tools. You can browse the content table or search by subject and grade level. Free weekly updates available.

CanTeach Resources for Educators
http://www.track0.com/canteach/index.html

A well organized source of searchable elementary lesson plans, resources and links with a Canadian focus.

Classroom Connect's Connected Teacher
http://connectedteacher.classroom.com/lessonplans/
lessonplans.asp

A very good collection of lesson plans and activities for Math, Sciences, Language Arts/Languages, American History, Social Studies organized into two divisions K-6 and 7-12. Also includes links to other sites that have been reviewed and recommended by Gleason Sackmann, Internet education expert extraordinaire and founder of Nethappenings. Highly recommended.

Cool Teaching Lessons and Units
http//www.cl.ais.net/rlevine/coolunits.htm

Here's a resource for K-12 teachers who wish to find quality ready-made units and lessons for all subjects, or who wish to develop their own units. This site emphasizes WebQuests and Problem-Based Learning as unit formats, but links include other forms of lessons, tutorials and projects. Even if teachers have one or no computer in their classrooms, these units can be of much help.

Core Knowledge
http://www.coreknowledge.org

Pre-K to 8 lesson plans and units developed by teachers in Core Knowledge schools and presented at recent national Core Knowledge conferences.

The Daybook
http//www.daybook.org

A teacher created searchable database of online lesson plans. You can print out new lessons to use right away! Any teacher can easily submit by filling out the online form. The Daybook is currently featuring a selection of K-7 subjects.

Discovery Channel School Lesson Plans
http://school.discovery.com/lessonplans/

An excellent site for finding detailed lesson plans for the classroom. Divided into two divisions, grades K-6 and grades 7-12. The K-6 lessons are created especially for elementary school teachers, emphasizing major K-6 topics such as early explorers, basic science, and world history and culture. Lesson plans include audio files for vocabulary pronunciation and definitions, questions for students, links to other websites and activities. You can also download all the resources in one file for easy printing. A great first stop for lesson planning!

ED's Oasis K-12 Teacher Resources
http://www.classroom.com/edsoasis/

Browse the collection of winning entries in the ED's Oasis Master Search Contest. Fantastic lesson plans organized in four divisions: K-3; 4-6; 7-9; and 10-12. Be sure to check out other resources on this site such as the e-mail list, message board, interviews, project and contest calendars and teacher resources.

Education Planet
http://educationplanet.com/

A well designed search engine returns your queries with resources such as lesson plans, websites, software, videos, maps, supplies, books and news. Well annotated search answers are also categorized according to grade level, problems, projects, resources, activities, genre, games, puzzles and more.

Education World Lesson Planning Center
http://www.education-world.com/a_lesson/archives/

Browse over 100 original, well written lesson planning articles written by the staff at Education World. Sign up for newsletters to keep you informed of the latest lesson plans, new education categories, topics of interest and more.

Eduniverse.com
http://www.eduniverse.com/

A collection of over 2,000 K-12 lesson plans from the Intel Applying Computers in Education (ACE) Project. Lesson plans are searchable by subject, grade level and keywords. The top award winning lesson plans can be viewed separately in chart form in alphabetical order or by state.

The Gateway to Educational Materials
http://www.thegateway.org/

Sponsored by the U.S. Department of Education's National Library of Education, The Gateway to Educational Materials contains over 10,000 education resources and materials found on various federal, state, university, non-profit, and commercial Internet sites. Browse through the curriculum database lists by subject, keyword or search by subject, keyword, title, or grade level.

Homework Central
http://www.bigchalk.com/

Part of the Big Chalk site, this is a huge section with over 100,000 links and over 10,000 subjects. Organized by categories and a very fast search engine. Head over to the Lesson Plan Archives for a detailed list of lessons.

Kathy Schrock's Guide for Educators
http://school.discovery.com/schrockguide/

Well known Internet education expert Kathy Schrock, maintains and updates this well organized list of sites daily. The sites here can be used to add to your lesson planning and professional development. Sign up for the Site of the School Day (S.O.S.) e-mail mailing list from September until June and receive an introduction to a new site. An easy way to stay up-to-date with the Internet.

The Lesson Plans Page
http://www.lessonplanspage.com/

Over 900 lessons searchable by subject and grade. Some very innovative lessons can be found here. Also available is a newsletter to inform you whenever new lesson plans are added to the site.

LessonPlanZ.com
http://lessonplanz.com/

Search or browse over 3,500 lesson plans. Lessons are also categorized as Pre-K, K-2, 3-5, 6-9, and 9-12 themes and subjects. This is an extensive hand picked and reviewed lesson plan site. Features include a Quick Lesson Plan link to the categories of Holidays/Seasonal, New Lesson Plan Additions, Top Rated Lesson Plans and Random. Other wonderful resources include links to Worksheets and Printable pages, Songs and Poems, Recipes, Message Boards and a Free Newsletter. A definite keeper for finding lesson resources.

Lesson Stop
http://www.youthline-usa.com/lessonstop/

Seven subject area pages, linked to 500 web sites, organized by topic and grade level will give you access to thousands of lesson plans. A free bimonthly "The Lesson Stop Newsletter" contains more online lesson plan sites for teachers. A popular and innovative feature found here is R.S.V.P.- Requests, S'il Vous Plait. It's a way subscribers to the newsletter can ask for help in finding the lessons they need. Answers are posted in future newsletters as time permits.

Lightspan
http://www.lightspan.com/

Over 115,000 links to up-to-date resources can be searched here using the Learning Search engine. Search by grade (K-12), keyword or by topic. Results are quickly returned as website reviews, encyclopedia articles, learning activities, lesson plans, home activities and projects. Resources are individually selected by Lightspan's education specialists. Highly recommended.

Links for K-12 Teachers
http://www.memphis-schools.k12.tn.us/admin/tlapages/k12links.htm

A well thought out collection of wonderful sites for teachers of all grades. There are hidden gems here that I haven't found anywhere else.

Longfellow Links
http://www.col.k12.me.us/lon/lonlinks/

Grade three teacher and technology coordinator Doug DeCamilla at Longfellow Elementary School in Brunswick, Maine, USA has collected, created and maintained more than 1,000 websites for grades K-5. Take a look.

Mountain Brook City Schools Technology Integration
http://www.mtnbrook.k12.al.us/tech/tech.htm

The Mountain Brook City Schools Integration Pages are an extensive collection of K-6 sites organized by subjects and grade levels. The pages were created by taking their existing curriculum and finding sites to enhance it.

Mr. K's Links 2 Learning 4 Educators
http://www.geocities.com/Athens/Column/9885/

I really enjoy seeing educational sites evaluated by letter grades. Teacher Mr. K does just that! This is a uniquely organized gateway site for educators. Links, arranged in nearly 70 very intuitive categories, are identified, briefly described, and subjectively rated for ease of use. Ease of navigating the site is a definite plus to preview the nearly 5,000 links available here.

Proteacher
http://www.proteacher.com/lessonplans.html

K-6 lesson plans searchable by subject or by category.

Reach Every Child
http://www.reacheverychild.com/

Hall of Fame and award winning teacher Alan Haskvitz has designed this site with over 5,000 free and inexpensive resources he's collected and used in his classroom over the years. It covers all subject areas and is changed on a regular basis to reflect current events and the calendar.

SMILE Science and Mathematics Initiative for Learning Enhancement
http://www.iit.edu/~smile/

Over 800 lesson plans available grades 3-12 in the areas of Biology, Chemistry, Mathematics and Physics. Lessons are divided into categories for easy searching and are available on the website.

Teachers@Work
http://teachers.work.co.nz/

Kia Ora, Welcome to this searchable database of 3,000 reviewed websites sorted into curriculum areas from New Zealand. To get included in this database, sites must meet 23 quality criteria regarding layout, language level, content and educational approach. Each site receives a content rating out of 5 (5+ being the highest rating) and a presentation rating out of 5. There is also an age rating for each site. Ratings are well annotated and well written.

Teachers.net Lesson Bank
http://teachers.net/lessons/

Over 1,500 teacher-submitted lesson plans are available here in a searchable collection for use with students in preschool through secondary school. Sorted by grade level and curriculum categories, the collection easily allows teachers to find the information they need about lessons and activities. And if you can't find a lesson, just submit it to the Lesson Plan Request Board. This is a great place not only to find resources, but to share your own.

Trackstar
http://trackstar.scrtec.org/

The South Central Regional Technology in Education Consortium TrackStar guides are a set of very complete web based lesson plans for K-12 students. They are searchable by keyword, author, themes and standards, subject and category and track ID. This site also allows teachers to open an account and build their own lessons online. Other features include making quizzes and web pages of the lesson. Great ideas can be found here from very innovative teachers. Take a visit and feel free to e-mail the authors and add to the lessons.

YES I Can! Science
http://yesican.yorku.ca/home/

A database of Science lessons for K-12 and Science expeditions. Searchable by keyword, grade, curriculum strand and cluster.

Theme Sites

A to Z Teacher Stuff Thematic Units Index
http://atozteacherstuff.com/themes/

Great site for building your K-12 curriculum units. Categories are evaluated based on grades and division for easy searching.

Berit's Sites for Children Holidays & Seasons
http://www.beritsbest.com/14498.shtml

Berit Erickson has assembled a fine list of Holiday and Seasons sites for children under 12. Each site is reviewed, given a rating out of 5 and ranked for the week. Regular e-mail updates are also available.

College of Library and Information Science
http://www.libsci.sc.edu/miller/unitlink.htm

Collaboratively created primary thematic units for a course assignment.

Community Learning Network
http://www.cln.org/themes_index.html

The theme pages here are a combination of curricular links and instructional materials links focused on a K-12 topic. Good information for teachers.

Connecting Students Through Themes and Units
http://www.connectingstudents.com/themes/

Detailed themes and units for Language Arts, Science and Social Studies K-12 as well as a Miscellaneous section which includes Pre-K to 2. Great site.

The Educator's Toolkit
http://www.eagle.ca/~matink

Very extensive list of resources for Themes, Mini-Themes and Holidays.

Gander Academy
http://www.stemnet.nf.ca/CITE/themes.html

A list of resources based on themes commonly taught at the primary and elementary levels grades K-6. Each of the over one hundred fifty theme pages contain a list of links to resources, lesson plans and curriculum ideas.

Georgia Dept of Ed. Teacher Resource Center
http://www.glc.k12.ga.us/passwd/trc/

Click on the Themes and Topics link for a cornucopia of wonderful resources organized by grade cluster K-2, 3-5, 6-8 and 9-12. Excellent first stop.

Instructional Technology Davis School District
http://www.davis.k12.ut.us/etc/themes.htm

A well laid out chart of predominantly Science and Social Studies topics.

Learning Page.com
http://www.learningpage.com/index.html

Download theme sheets in Adobe Acrobat PDF file for grades K-2. Themes include Oceans, Zoo Animals, Dinosaurs, Insects/Spiders. Regular updates.

The Learning Space
http://www.learningspace.org/instruct/primary/sites/seasonal.html

Primary themes organized by months of the year. Lots of them.

Surfing the Net with Kids
http://www.surfnetkids.com/

Syndicated newspaper columnist, Barb J. Feldman posts a collection of websites dealing with a particular topic. Websites are rated and annotated. Sign up for her free biweekly newsletter.

Sites For Beginning Teachers

ADPRIMA: Toward the Best
http://www.adprima.com/index.html

The ADPRIMA site contains detailed, practical, straightforward information that new teachers need to know about - planning, curriculum, instruction, students, classroom management, lesson planning, teaching methods, assertive discipline, study skills, thinking skills, and a whole lot more.

Association for Supervision and Curriculum Development
http://www.ascd.org/

A number of very helpful articles for beginning teachers are found here. Read what Patricia Wasley has to say about building and using a repertoire of teaching strategies and techniques, to help all students succeed in her article "Teaching Worth Celebrating" at:
http://www.ascd.org/readingroom/edlead/9905/extwasley.html

Invaluable tips for experienced and new teachers appear in Karen Rasmussen's article "Make It Great: Tips for a Successful, Fulfilling School Year" at:
http://www.ascd.org/readingroom/edupdate/1999/1aug.html

Advice from three award-winning veteran teachers on how to set a positive tone for learning that will persist for the rest of the year can be read in Jamie Sawatzky's article "Making a Good Start" at:
http://www.ascd.org/readingroom/edupdate/1997/1sep.html

Beginning Teachers' Handbook
http://www.bctf.bc.ca/career/beginning/handbook/

From the British Columbia Teachers' Federation in the province of British Columbia Canada, comes this fantastic, practical and very complete resource. Here can be found chapters on classroom management (what works and what doesn't) establishing a positive environment, communicating with parents/guardians, teaching strategies, teaching tips (homework dos and don'ts), taking care of yourself (perfectionism and surviving). Highly recommended!

Beginning Teachers' Tool Box
http://www.inspiringteachers.com/

Click on the TIPS section and read articles on "Getting Ready for the School Year", "Beginning of the Year Packet", "Time Saving Tips", "Classroom Management Tips." For more resources, head over to Thoughts For New Teachers, or go to the Message Boards and ask a question in the Beginning Teacher Message Board or e-mail a message to Ask Our Mentor.

Elementary School Teachers
http://k-6educators.about.com/education/k-6educators/mbody.htm

Click on the link to the New Teachers section for links to tips and articles.

Kim's Korner For Teacher Talk
http://www.angelfire.com/ks/teachme/

Go to the Classroom Management link to get some great ideas on the following topics: Tips for Getting Organized, Ideas for Bulletin Boards, Inexpensive Items--Where to Get Them, Icebreakers and Energizers, Review Games, How to Simplify the Grading Work Load, Activities for the First Days of School.

New-Teacher.com
http://www.new-teacher.com/

Here's a resource site for first-year teachers, and anyone who thinks they'd like to be an educator someday. There's information, inspiration, and tools to become an effective teacher.

The New Teachers' Corner
http://www.microsoft.com/education/mctn/newteacher/default.asp

The New Teachers' Corner is a place where first-time teachers can find help for their biggest classroom challenges as well as quick, practical tips they can use from Day One. There's advice from seasoned pros, inspiration from peers and a diary of a new teacher. The Lifesavers' section with ideas such as end of the year projects, getting organized, tricky transitions are invaluable.

Teacher Talk, Volume 1, Issue 2
http://education.indiana.edu/cas/tt/v1i2/table.html

Good short articles for beginning teachers and the first day of school. Take the questionnaire "What is your classroom management profile?" and determine your classroom management profile. You may be surprised!

Teachers Helping Teachers
http://www.pacificnet.net/~mandel/

A lot of tips from fellow teachers. Check out the Classroom Management link and other resources. Post a question in the very active guest book/forum.

Teachers.Net Beginning Teachers ChatBoard
http://teachers.net/mentors/beginning_teachers/

Here's a very popular place for beginning teachers to network with other colleagues, share stories and seek the knowledge needed to teach well.

TeachNet.org
http://teachnet.org/home/home.htm

Head straight over to the New Teacher Helpline and read everything! If you still need more info, go to the message boards and ask any of the number of teacher specialists a question in their message board. A response to your question is guaranteed within 72 hours. A great place for any teacher.

U.S. Department of Education
http://www.ed.gov/pubs/FirstYear/

"What to Expect Your First Year of Teaching" contains a number of tips on such topics as Tips and Strategies from First-Year Teachers, The Kids, Veteran Teachers Talk, Final Thoughts and Additional Resources, and A Checklist of Tips. After all these years, I still agree with the piece of advice a veteran teacher is quoted as saying i.e. "be yourself." This publication is also available in Portable Document Format (PDF) [257K] for downloading.

Sites For Substitute Teachers

Proteacher.net
http://www.proteacher.net/

Share ideas with fellow substitute teachers on this message board.

The Substitute Teacher Homepage
http://my.voyager.net/garmar/default.htm

One of the best sites on the Internet for substitute teachers. Covers substitute and teacher tips, (yes, tips from the substitute to the teacher to make both jobs run better). Includes an extensive archive of tips, great time killer suggestions, stories, quotes, links, polls and wages. Highly recommended!

Substitute Teaching Institute
http://subed.usu.edu/bear.html

The mission of The Substitute Teaching Institute at Utah State University, Utah, USA is to revolutionize the role of substitute teachers into an opportunity for educational excellence. The Institute researches substitute teaching issues, including training and managing substitutes. A good place to visit and take a look at their research, handbooks and tips.

Substitute TEACHING -Tricks of the Trade-
http://www.av.qnet.com/~rsturgn/index.htm

A well written book (available online or by separate order) on what it's like to be a substitute teacher. Very useful appendix on power tips. Good links to other sources of information.

Works4Me Tips Library
http://www.nea.org/helpfrom/growing/works4me/relate/subs.html

Tips to help out substitute teachers with lesson, seating plans and little extras.

Primary Sites Grades Pre-K-3

Gareth Pitchford's Primary Resources
http://www.primaryresources.co.uk/

From the United Kingdom comes this invaluable resource of free, ready to use ideas, resources, worksheets and lesson plans. Some of the worksheets are in PDF files which can be read with an Adobe's Acrobat Reader on your computer. There are a lot of wonderful resources here. Help the site grow by sending in your lesson ideas, worksheets and resources. Well worth a stop.

Kinder Korner
http://geocities.com/Heartland/Hollow/1213/

It's not hard to see why Kinder Korner for grades Pre-K to 2 is a top rated primary site. There is a Back To School Section with resources such as First Day Checklists, Month to Month Themes and Beginning of the Year Assessment; a section on Thematic Units, a bookstore with links to resources and how to use the activities with your students, a Kinder Korner mailing list (past issues of the newsletter are available online) and links to other primary resources, sites and more. This Korner should be in every teacher's classroom.

Learning Page.com
http://www.learningpage.com/index.html

K-2 worksheets available here for the alphabet (print and cursive), calendar (days of the week and months of the year), money, time, measure (in imperial and metric measurment systems) and numbers.

Mrs. Hall's 1st Grade Class
http://mrshall.cjb.net/

Grade 1 was never like this! Read Mrs. Hall's lesson plans, grade 1 curriculum from previous years, projects ideas and links to other grade 1 classes.

Loogootee Elementary West
http//www.siec.k12.in.us/~west/index.html

K-3 school Loogootee Elementary West in Loogootee, Indiana, USA has a number of Internet projects, activities, articles and resources developed by staff and students. Visit them and see how they are integrating the Internet into the classroom curriculum. Take the time to read web editor Tammy Payton's magazine articles. You'll be glad you did.

Mrs. Gray's Second Grade Classroom
http://www.genevaschools.org/austinbg/class/gray/index.htm

This second grade classroom at Spencer Elementary in Geneva, Ohio, U.S.A. showcases their Internet and Classroom Projects. Here you'll find artwork, stories, research papers, links, photos of projects and pets, recycled pets, dinosaur dioramas, experiments, graphs, charts, surveys, online quizzes, book reports, copies of their 100 e-mails and postcards, digital photos of Giant Silk moths and two generations of butterflies, plus lots more!

Perpetual Preschool
http://www.perpetualpreschool.com/

A must visit site for any Kindergarten or grade 1 teacher. A great resource.

Susan Silverman Second Grade
http//comsewogue.k12.ny.us/~ssilverman/class99/index.html

Grade 2 teacher and Franklin Institute Online Fellow Susan Silverman of Clinton Avenue Elementary Port Jefferson Station, New York, USA shares her many wonderful projects, webfolios, links and resources on this fun website.

Teaching Ideas for Primary Teachers
http://www.teachingideas.co.uk/

Another great site from the United Kingdom. Designed for teachers who teach primary-age children (i.e. age 5 to 11), this site has well written lesson plans, is easy to use and has other features such as an option to download the entire site for a small fee, and a place for teachers to relax in a staffroom complete with a a notice board, highly addictive teacher games and even a dance area.

Elementary Sites Grades 4-6

4th and 5th Grade Student Research Resources
http://www.geocities.com/EnchantedForest/Tower/1217/

There's a section here for students and a link to a teachers' section containing resources by subjects. Resources for grades 1-3 and 6-8 can also be accessed.

6th Grade Treasure Trove
http://www.occdsb.on.ca/~proj1615/index.htm

Grade 6 teacher and Franklin Institute Online Fellow Karen Walkowiak at Holy Redeemer Catholic School in Kanata, Ontario, Canada has created this 6th Grade Treasure Trove as a cyberhaven for 6th grade teachers. It's her way of being able to network with other 6th grade teachers around the world, share ideas online, share and gain teaching tips, and use the Internet to enhance classroom curriculum. If you teach grade 6, surf over here as soon as you can!

Mrs. Seagraves' QUEST Class
http://www.geocities.com/Athens/Atrium/5924/index.html

Mrs. Seagraves teaches an elementary gifted program called QUEST in Montgomery, Alabama, USA to students in grades K-6. This site features individual student pages showcasing their work, several complete units for teachers, and lots of information about their classroom including Internet projects, field trips, and their desktop publishing business "QUEST Graphics." At this site you can create a virtual pond, play garden concentration, and lots of other neat games. I found great innovative units here for my own grade 5 class.

W. C. Walker Elementary
http://www.okaloosa.k12.fl.us/walker

Walker Elementary's website provides great teacher, parent, and student resources focused on Pre-K through 5th grade. Many resources updated regularly with sites reviewed for appropriateness and value. Provides links to lesson plans, online math practice, technology how to's, parenting and safe school information, fun and much more. A well organized and useful site.

Middle School Sites Grades 7-8

A Cybrary for Middle School and Beyond
http://www.geocities.com/Athens/Academy/6617/index.html

Well organized links for Middle School students and teachers.

Kentucky Migrant Technology Project
http://www.migrant.org/

One of the best places on the Internet that has the entire middle school curricula freely accessible to any and all students, parents and teachers. Select from over 29 online courses covering subject matter across the core curriculum areas of Math, English, Science, Social Studies, Arts and Humanities, and Practical Living in grades 6-12. The courses link to relevant educational websites that support the online instruction making the online classes totally web-based for text, tests, and teacher-student interaction. Courses are organized similarly to a regular school course, taught with daily lessons and activities followed by online quizzes and exams. Anyone can use these courses - from teachers needing lesson plans and suitable websites to students wanting to make up a lost credit over the summer. Highly recommended.

MiddleSchool
http://www.middleschool.com/

Great resource sections here for teachers and administrators. The Student Behavior Lab provides very comprehensive research, information, programs, and interventions to help you deal with behavior and help make your school a productive learning environment. Well written and useful articles for administrators on dealing with low staff morale and job satisfaction and how to turn it around. There are also links to subject resources and to other middle school resources.

MiddleWeb
http://www.middleweb.com/

Everything you wanted to know about Middle School and more is here on this award winning website. Catch up on the news about middle grades, student and teacher successes, standard based reform. Find curriculum resources including teaching strategies. Read about middle schools that are raising student achievement. Click on links to a collection of important resources covering reform, assessment, evaluation standards, charter schools, grouping, tracking, grade retention, parent involvement, public partnerships, professional development for teachers, urban schools and at-risk students, other useful stuff and even some fun. If you teach Middle School, this is the place to go.

Middle School Language Arts Site
http://students.resa.net/stoutcomputerclass/la.htm

Middle School Mathematics Site
http://students.resa.net/stoutcomputerclass/math.htm

Wonderful integrated lesson plans using the Internet.

Midlink Magazine
http://www.cs.ucf.edu/~MidLink/

National Technology Teacher of the Year Caroline McCullen, has developed MidLink Magazine to support educators all over the world as they inspire their students ages 8-18 to write and publish their work. Since 1994, MidLink Magazine, known as "the Digital Magazine for Kids, by Kids," has been an award-winning online magazine or "zine". The mission of MidLink Magazine is to highlight exemplary work from the most creative classrooms around the globe.

This award-winning, non-profit project is supported by SAS in School, the North Carolina State University College of Education and Psychology, and the Computer Science Department of the University of Central Florida, USA.

Millard Central Middle School
http://www.esu3.org/web/mcms.html

The Millard Central Middle School in Omaha, Nebraska, USA website provides students and teachers easy access to high quality, safe resources appropriate to Middle School curriculum. Special features include search tools, curriculum links, current events resources, and curriculum pathfinders, which are designed to supplement specific units of study. Many of the school web pages have been developed by students.

Multimedia Applications on a Shoe-String Budget
http://library.thinkquest.org/50001/

Here is a well thought out, well planned and well designed site to show Middle School teachers with limited resources how to teach multimedia applications and technology skills to Middle School students while also integrating these tools into classroom curricula. The resources here are great. There are sections on Technology Lesson Plan Format, Steps for Integrating Multimedia into Classroom Instruction, Units to Teach Technology Skills, Units to Reinforce Technology and Core Content Skills, Lesson Plans/Units by Curriculum Areas and Teacher Resources. If you're teaching technology skills, this is for you.

National Association of Elementary School Prinicipals
http://www.naesp.org/

NAESP has grown to become the most powerful voice of Pre-K-8 principals across the United States and around the world. If you're an administrator or want to become one, you'll want to visit this site.

National Middle School Association (NMSA)
http://www.nmsa.org/

Established in 1973, National Middle School Association (NMSA) serves as a voice for professionals, parents, and others interested in improving the educational experiences and developmental needs of young adolescents (youth 10-15 years of age). Great resources and links to even more.

High School Sites Grades 9-12

David Levin's Learning@Web.Sites
http://www.ecnet.net/users/gdlevin/home.html

This site is intended primarily for senior high school educators who would like to enhance their curriculum and instruction using the Internet. Students will also find the site to be a rich online resource guide.

High School Hub
http://highschoolhub.org/

A noncommercial gateway to free online academic resources for high school students. It features interactive learning activities, an ongoing poetry contest, student artwork, a reference collection, college information, and subject guides.

Kentucky Migrant Technology Project
http://www.migrant.org/

One of the best sites around that has the entire high school curricula freely accessible to any and all students, parents and teachers. Highly recommended.

The National Association of Secondary School Principals
http://www.nassp.org/

The National Association of Secondary School Principals (NASSP) serves leaders in middle level and high schools, including administrators, teachers, students, and others interested in education and the welfare of today's youth.

Secondary School Educators
http://7-12educators.about.com/education/7-12educators/mbody.htm

An extensive list of subject links, articles and resources for high school teachers brought to you by a "real live" guide. An interactive chat board is also available to discuss current issues in the secondary school system.

College and University Sites

2001 Colleges, College Scholarships, And Financial Aid Page
http://www.college-scholarships.com/

This 2001 Colleges, College Scholarships, and Financial Aid page is designed to offer college bound students, parents, and counselors easy access to information on colleges and universities throughout the United States, free college scholarship and financial aid searches, information on SAT, ACT, GRE and GMAT, TOEFL examinations, MBA programs, and more. Among the extensive resources included here are an online directory of college and university admissions office e-mail addresses and telephone numbers, college scholarship and financial aid office e-mail addresses, and links to the home pages and online applications of more than a thousand colleges and universities.

The College Board
http://www.collegeboard.org/

The College Board is a national, nonprofit membership association dedicated to preparing, inspiring, and connecting students to college and opportunity. This site will help you get the SAT question of the day, every day, 7 days a week, register for the SAT and get test dates, search and apply for colleges, request CSS/Financial Aid, sign up for workshops and more.

Deliberations on Teaching and Learning
http://www.lgu.ac.uk/deliberations/

Deliberations is designed to act as a resource for educational developers, librarians, academic staff and managers in education. Resources include a forum for readers to discuss and develop ideas, identify resources that will aid their work, evaluated case studies of teaching and learning in subject discipline areas, contact lists of staff interested in similar work, extracts of related published articles, commentary on case studies and articles contributed by readers, book reviews, annotated bibliographies, links to related resources and relevant publishers. Content is searchable using pull down menus.

eCollege.com
http://www.ecollege.com/

Students can search for thousands of courses online from hundreds of colleges and universities by discipline, state and institution. Resources here for educators include help in incorporating the Internet into their courses, teaching online, enhancing course content and keeping up-to-date with an e-newsletter.

Embark.com
http//www.embark.com

Here's an online guide for students and educators to learn about and connect with educational and career opportunities. The website has information on nearly 6,000 accredited higher education institutions, profiles on over 1,000 careers and majors, comprehensive financial aid data, and online applications.

Study Guides And Strategies
http//www.iss.stthomas.edu/studyguides

Study Guides and Strategies is a website devoted to improving students' success in learning. Contains over 70 pages of practical suggestions, as for time and stress management; basic skills in reading, writing, and classroom participation; test preparation and test taking from the University of St. Thomas' Learning Center in Minnesota, USA.

World Lecture Hall
http://www.utexas.edu/world/lecture/index.html

The World Lecture Hall (WLH) contains links to pages created by faculty worldwide who are using the Web to deliver university-level academic courses in any language. Useful links to other distance education sites.

Writing And Printing Your Thesis Or Dissertation
http//www.msue.msu.edu/aee/dissthes/guide.htm

This non-commercial practical guide has been created to assist in the crafting, implementing and defending of a graduate school thesis or dissertation. It includes a variety of strategies, suggestions and advice covering every stage of the thesis or dissertation project.

Chapter 3

Sites That Motivate, Engage And Stimulate Students (And Educators)

"A mind stretched to a new idea never goes back to its original dimension."

Oliver Wendell Holmes

There are times on dreary Monday mornings, or on long Friday afternoons or when an emergency comes up and a substitute is called in, that an activity is needed to motivate, to engage and to stimulate the class. The sites here go a long way to helping the busy educator with those times. They have been chosen to address a variety of learning styles, grade levels and abilities. The sites have been arranged by subjects and grade levels. I have also included whether the information would also be of benefit to parents and teachers.

The recommended grade levels indicated for each site is only a recommendation. Sometimes the reading material may be too difficult for some grades, but the information is suitable to grade level standards and expectations. Student abilities vary from school to school, district to district. Educators should always check the sites in advance before having students access them. Although this is sometimes difficult for busy educators to do, the time honored adage of always checking your equipment before a class applies even more to the World Wide Web and the Internet. The Web is dynamic. Sites change, links become outdated and the material you were once looking for may have moved! To avoid any surprises, it's always a good idea to see what's on the sites a day or two before your class.

Here are some ideas that Louisa Howerow, former teacher-librarian and now a vice-principal in London, Ontario, Canada has used to introduce the Internet into her school. These ideas do not pertain to a specific site, but are applicable to many:

• set up a game club in your school and encourage students to enter contests. This is a great, fun way to promote research.

• print out Math problems and pass them on to the Math club, to the gifted class, to the teacher who has pupils who need enrichment, to the teacher who is looking to enrich the program, to the resource teacher who needs something different.

• set up a research corner in the library with the question of the week and the appropriate research tools; have a place where students can place their answers; have a draw and prizes.

• announce questions on the public address system. Individual pupils, groups, or classes can submit answers and are eligible for prizes. If there is enough lead-time, announce questions in your newsletters. Encourage children to work with parents to find solutions.

• as a teacher-librarian, pass on information from the Internet to all teachers. Teachers who are reluctant to use the Internet will do so if you present the activity as a partners-in-action project or you volunteer to take a group of students and work with them.

• as a teacher-librarian, pass on information to parents (include websites in class newsletters, in school newsletters, in the home and school newsletters) and pass on information to students (bookmarks, bulletin board displays).

• announce games and results of games in newsletters.

• have students record new words from sites and include them in their journal or personal dictionaries. This database of words which they've now created, can be used to make word searches, crossword puzzles, spelling tests, games of charades and "draw that word" games, in stories, essays, acrostic poems. Include them as a "word of the day" on the blackboard, in morning announcements and in newsletters sent home to parents.

- organize a parent night to show parents how the Internet and computers are used in the class and can be used at home. Set up some of the game sites, have available research tools, and encourage parents and children to "play".

- etymology sites, what happened on your birthday sites, and rhyming dictionary are great sites for students doing autobiographies on themselves. Use the information found on these sites to make a booklet or a poster that defines them. For example, my name means, what happened on my birthday, great words that rhyme with my name (and reflect who I am). Make a similar card or booklet for a friend, or for a parent on Mother's Day or Father's Day.

- a great teacher is a teacher that never stops learning. Contact other teachers via e-mail; learn from your colleagues; share your ideas with others. E-mail interaction is low-cost, time sensitive and can be adapted to your specific professional development needs.

I highly recommend the following websites for more curriculum integration suggestions. The ideas in these seven websites can be used for the sites in this chapter and other quality educational sites.

Hazel Jobe (gr. K-12)
http://www.marshall-es.marshall.k12.tn.us/jobe/sites1.html

Hazel has posted a vast collection of ideas from her collaborative teacher sharing project. These web based lessons and ideas are organized into the following grade levels: K-6, 7-12 and K-12.

Joan Marie Brown (gr. 6-8)
http://www-personal.umd.umich.edu/~jobrown/

Joan has integrated lesson plans with Math and Language Arts websites.

Challenge Lessons for the K-12 Classroom (gr. K-12)
http://www.challenge.state.la.us/k12act/

A collection of lesson plans, unit plans and collaborative projects developed by Louisiana teachers geared to the use of the Internet in classroom lessons.

Cyberguides: Teacher Guides & Student Activities (gr. K-12)
http://www.sdcoe.k12.ca.us/score/cyberguide.html

The Schools of California Online Resources for Education (SCORE) site offers great practical lesson plans, novel studies divided by grade level, tips and suggestions for teaching Language Arts using the Internet. These guides are grouped according to grades K-3 , 6-8 and 9-12. Each Cyber Guide contains a Student and Teacher Edition, Statement of Objectives, a Task and a Process by which it may be completed and a Rubric for Assessing the Quality of the Product. They were produced at the San Diego County Office of Education and were funded by the California Technology Assistance Program. Click on the following link: **http://www.sdcoe.k12.ca.us/score/cla.html** for Math, Science, History and Social Science sites.

McGraw-Hill School Division (gr. K-8)
http://www.mmhschool.com/misc/toc1.html

Web-linked lesson plans available here for Reading and Language Arts, Mathematics, Social Studies and Music.

TrackStar guides and lesson plans (Early childhood-College)
http://scrtec.org/track/

The South Central Regional Technology in Education Consortium TrackStar guides are a set of complete web based lesson plans on the World Wide Web.

Art

Art For Kids (gr. K-12)
http://artforkids.tqn.com/

An extensive list of Art resources by seasoned About.com guide Tracy Pearson.

Art Kids Rule (gr. K-16)
http://artkidsrule.com/

Great fun activities, resources, tutorials, lesson plans, artist forums. This site will appeal to kids of all ages and abilities. Click on the Art Arcades and create your own play, choose the stars and assign their own lines.

Cards (All)
http://www.cardcentral.net

This mega card site is one of the largest virtual postcard and greeting card index sites on the Internet with links to over 1,500 card sites. You can browse the sites alphabetically, look at them by special features, special occasions or check out the cool sites. Whatever way you choose, you'll find that perfect card here. Show students how to send cards to show appreciation, birthday and holiday celebrations. These cards also make great "warm fuzzies!" Use information from "Today in History" sites such celebrating what happened in the year someone was born. Also check out Blue Mountain **http://www. bluemountain.com/** one of the first greeting card sites on the Internet.

Daryl Cagle's Professional Cartoonists Index (gr. 6-12)
http://www.cagle.com/

An extensive resource of information looking behind the scenes of cartoonists. Includes a teacher's guide. Mature themes in current events are covered here.

Educational Web Adventures (gr. K-12)
http://www.eduweb.com/adventure.html

Adventures and more adventures with wildlife Art, making your own masterpieces, being an Art detective, exploring a painting from the inside out and more. This website is the main gateway to all kinds of great adventures.

Eileen's Camp Crafts and Other Fun Things (gr. Pre-K-8) (Parents and Teachers)
http//www.chadiscrafts.nu/fun/

This is a site that features crafts and links for beadie animals, clay, braiding and many original projects. Includes a guide to supplies and resources plus fun pages for games and educational sites for children.

Joseph Wu's Origami Page (gr. 4-12)
http://www.origami.vancouver.bc.ca/

Learn origami from this master. A fabulous and top rated origami site with lots of models, illustrations, explanations. Links and other resources.

KinderArt (gr. K-12) (Parents and Teachers)
http://www.kinderart.com/

The largest collection of free Art lessons and Art education information on the Internet. Your complete all-in-one Art education resource.

The Refrigerator Art Contest (gr. K-12)
http://www.artcontest.com/

Each week, the producers of The Refrigerator Art Contest pick five pictures to display on their site in The Competition section. Then they're voted on by you.

World Wide Arts Resources (gr. 4-12)
http://wwar.com/

This is a gateway to huge resources to artists, museums, Art history and more.

ESL/Foreign Languages

Core French (Teachers)
http://www.lled.educ.ubc.ca/mled/frcorlnk.htm

From the Department of Language and Literacy Education, at the University of British Columbia comes this invaluable resource for French teachers.

Dave's ESL Café (Teachers)
http://www.eslcafe.com/

One of the most popular ESL sites on the Internet.

Learn English (Teachers)
http://www.englishday.com/

Solve crossword puzzles online, read silly jokes, take interactive tests, find the hidden word, do a word search and other activities to learn English.

TESL/TEFL/TESOL/ESL/EFL/ESOL Links (Teachers) (Students)
http://www.aitech.ac.jp/~iteslj/links/

Over 5,800 links for students and teachers of English as a Second Language. Two very easy to read charts are set up: one for students and one for teachers. Includes self-study, crossword, Javascript quizzes, classroom games and much, much more. This site is optimized for speed and updated often.

The Language Course Finder (Teachers)
http//www.language-learning.net /

An online directory of language schools, listing more than 6,000 schools, 80 countries, 70 languages worldwide. Detailed search facilities enable website visitors to search for and find a program matching interests. Each institution is listed with full address details for direct contact. Also includes information on language learning/teaching materials, language tests and organizations.

Randall's ESL Cyber Listening Lab (Teachers)
http://www.esl-lab.com/index.htm

An interactive listening lab with easy, medium and difficult exercises.

Really Useful French Teaching Site (Teachers)
http://www.btinternet.com/~s.glover/S.Glover/languagesite/
Default.htm

A bilingual site offering exercises for the early teens, interactive exercises, useful teacher programs to create motivating mataterials, French grammar, simple practical ideas to get pupils speaking and writing. It is very useful.

Really Useful German Teaching Site (Teachers)
http://atschool.eduweb.co.uk/haberg/reallyusefulge/default.htm

The companion site to the Really Useful French Teaching Site, this site is also packed with good practical ideas. You can find useful ideas that work in the classroom, interactive programs, listening practice and more.

Say It In French (Teachers)
http://ambafrance.org/ALF/

A 30-minute game in French. You will be landing in Roissy-Charles-De-Gaulle airport in Paris. You have 6 hours to reach the Eiffel Tower and meet Mr. Langlois at the Eiffel restaurant for an important and pleasurable meal. Plugin required, but the effort is certainly worth it. Bon appétit!

Surfez le Net (Teachers)
http://www.learner.org/catalog/worldlangs/fiseries/surfez/

Surfez le Net is a list of annotated French websites. You can browse by subjects, including tourism, language, news, and entertainment. You can get lists of the most recently added sites, or search by site title or keyword. Surfez le Net's database contains information about more than 150 francophone websites and is updated twice a week.

Teachers of English to Speakers of Other Languages
(Teachers)
http://www.tesol.edu/

Great site for resources and news for TEOSL. Check out the Wandering The Web link. This column is a great source of teaching information.

Travlang (gr. 4-16) (Parents and Teachers)
http://www.travlang.com/

Find common expressions in over 70 foreign languages, links to over 7,000 different websites on the Internet relating to both foreign travel and language, a travel library, currency exchange which gives the latest exchange rates for foreign currencies, maps, phone information, calendars showing national holidays and more. Click on words and expressions to hear how they are spoken. This is an ideal source for students doing travel brochures or learning common language expressions of another country.

Vocabulary Training Exercies (Teachers)
http://www.vokabel.com/

Interactive language tests on all the basics in German, French, Spanish and English. Click your mother tongue link and start practicing.

Language Arts

Biography Maker (gr. 4-8)
http://www.bham.wednet.edu/bio/biomaker.htm

Step by step lessons to help students write biographies. Very useful.

Book Adventure (gr. K-8) (Parents and Teachers)
http://www.bookadventure.com/

Created by the Sylvan Learning Foundation and sponsored by well known educational associations and corporations, Book Adventure is a free, reading incentive program dedicated to encouraging kids in grades K-8 to read. Kids have more than 4,000 popular books to choose from. They can then take a quiz on each book read for prize incentives. Great resource for teachers to search for books by grade level, author, genre, reading level and then print out books as a reading list. Teachers can also set up their own class for quizzes. Great reading links and resources. Registration is required.

Channel One News (gr. 6-12)
http://www.teach1.com/

A detailed media literacy curriculum with lesson plans, worksheets and support materials you need to teach the news.

The Children's Literature Web Guide (Teachers)
http://www.ucalgary.ca/~dkbrown/

Links to author's websites, resources for K-12 teachers, book reviews.

CRAYON (gr. 4-14) (Parents and Teachers)
http://crayon.net/

CRAYON (Create Your Own Newspaper) is a personalized Internet news service. Here's a way to encourage even the most reluctant reader to read. Easy step by step instructions show students (and adults) how to create their own newspaper with links to news sources from the Internet. E-mail address is required. Younger children may need guidance due to links to tabloids.

Education by Design (gr. K-6)
(Parents and Teachers)
http://www.edbydesign.com

A fun site for kids. Play scrambler puzzles, (recommended) practice mathematical skills, publish stories, jokes, riddles, and poems online. Great reading, writing, spelling and special education tips for teachers and parents.

English Zone (gr. 3-6)
http://english-zone.com

Quick and easy worksheets, handouts, online exercises for interactive language lessons, exercises and quizzes. Learn about idioms, grammar, verbs and more. This site is packed with wonderful useful information and activities.

Kidbibs (gr. Pre-K-7) (Parents and Teachers)
http://www.kidbibs.com/

A resource site for reading. Great tips for parents and teachers on how to encourage reading. Detailed outlines on how to find great books for kids to read by age level. Links to reading websites for 4-8 and 9-12 year olds. There is also an extensive collection of awards you can personalize and print off for your students. Very easy and fun to use.

Kid's Mysteries (gr. 4-8)
http://www.TheCase.com/kids/

There are mysteries here to solve, scary stories to read, magic tricks to think about, and contests to enter. A new mystery every week.

Learn Vocabulary Syndicate (gr. 4-8)
http://www.syndicate.com/

Grade specific puzzles, comic strips, word games and many other ways to sharpen your skills. Use these quizzes to prepare students for the SAT.

Lights, Puppets, Action! (gr. 3-6)
http://www.childrensmuseum.org/

Turn pretend stories into online puppet shows in a few simple steps. Point and click to menus for your cast, plot, setting, music and animation. Great resources for teachers, including lesson plans, games and links to puppet sites.

Meet Authors and Illustrators (gr. K-10)
http://www.childrenslit.com/

Links to author's websites, Literature Annual Top Choice List, book reviews.

M-tech Worksheet Generator
http://www.mtech.on.ca/windex.html

Make free worksheets here. Vocabulary worksheets for scramble, chop, matching, fill in the blanks, mixed up paragraph exercises and more.

MysteryNet's Learning With Mysteries (Teachers)
http://www.mysterynet.com/learn/

Hook students on the craft of mystery reading and writing with lesson plans and ideas from this site. Includes useful sites, examples and discussions.

National Film Board of Canada (gr. K-5)
http://www.nfb.ca/Kids

Read a charming story with your primary students. Or have younger students partnered up with older ones. Interactive features encourage students to read.

National Council of Teachers of English (Teachers)
http://www.ncte.org/

An invaluable resource for grants, awards and the latest news for teachers of English and Language Arts K-12. Go to the archives and use the search function to get ideas for teaching a specific novel, short stories and poems.

Newslink (gr. 6-12)
http://cbc.ca/programs/sites/newslink.html

Newslink is a 15-minute news and current affairs teaching tool produced every day by CBC (Canadian Broadcast Corporation) Newsworld in Calgary, Alberta, Canada for Cable-in-the-Classroom. It combines the stories and information of the CBC's national and international news service with a lesson plan available on this site. You can find Newslink at 4:06 am Easter Time, 2:06 am Mountain Time. Make sure you program the VCR. All of the video in Newslink is copyright cleared for use in Canadian classrooms.

NoodleBib (gr. 6-12) (Teachers)
http://www.noodletools.com/noodlebib/

How do you cite a Web page? An online magazine article? This site will create a bibliography for you automatically.

Nursery Rhymes Coloring Pages (gr. Pre-K– 3)
http://www.EnchantedLearning.com/Rhymes.html

Dozens of rebus nursery rhymes in alphabetical order. Click on the picture for a coloring page and the rhyme. Then print them out for your class. Or have the class color them online. Also instructions for making a nursery rhyme coloring book, a scavenger hunt and information on teaching rhymes in your class.

The Online Books Page (gr. 3-12)
http://digital.library.upenn.edu/books/

Download the classics from this site. Here's a directory of books that can be freely read right on the Internet. It includes an index of thousands of online books, links to directories and archives of online texts and special exhibits.

Online Writing Lab from Purdue Univerisity (OWL) (gr. 4-12)
http://owl.english.purdue.edu/

Over 130 handouts. Links and resources on every aspect of writing.

Paradigm Online Writing Assistant (gr. 6-12)
http://www.powa.org/

Here's an interactive writer's guide and handbook. Great help for story, essay writing and documenting sources.

Personal Educational Press (gr. 1-4)
http://www.educationalpress.org/

This website turns your computer and printer into a printing press for free educational materials such as flashcards and game boards. This online tool runs directly off your browser - there are no plug-ins to install, no software to buy.

The Quotations Page (gr. 5-16)
http://www.starlingtech.com/quotes/

Use these quotes for class discussions. Have students research their favorite quotes and include them in their journals. Links to other quotation sites.

Shared Reading In Kindergarten (Teachers)
http://www.ertp.santacruz.k12.ca.us/srk/sr_homepage.html

A description and step-by-step lesson on shared reading. Includes a sample shared reading lesson, lesson plan template and links to related topics.

Star Wars The Magic of Myth (gr. 5-12)
http://www.nasm.edu/StarWars/sw-unit1.htm

See the behind the scenes magic in the making of the movie Star Wars from the Smithsonian National Air and Space Museum. Students will quickly appreciate the work that goes into the making of a movie of this magnitude.

TIME for Kids (gr. K-6)
http://www.timeforkids.com/

Weekly magazine for kids available in three editions: TIME For Kids: Big Picture Edition - Grades K-1, TIME For Kids: News Scoop Edition - Grades 2-3 and TIME For Kids: World Report Edition - Grades 4-6. Great site!

Vocabulary University (gr. 5-16)
http://www.vocabulary.com/

Features include grade level interactive word puzzles that help expand one's vocabulary such as puzzles using Latin & Greek roots, synonyms, antonyms analogies, thematic word puzzles. Quick lesson plans available for teachers.

Wacky World of Words (gr. K-12)
http://www.members.home.net/teachwell/

Includes great activities for the class such as Compound Clues, Words Within Words, Numbletters, Alpha-Spells, Fractured Fractions, Rhyming Buddies, A-Z Lists, Anagrams, Similes, Oxymorons, Mystery Word, and links to other sites. I was really intrigued by the Fractured Fractions activity. It combines language and math skills. You take a fraction of one word and add it with a fraction of another word to give you a new word. For example: take the first 1/2 of what + the last 3/5 of there, and you get the word where.

Weekly Reader (gr. Pre-K-6)
(Parents and Teachers)
http://www.weeklyreader.com

Site with an elementary student newspaper. Contains separate editions for Pre-kindergarten through grade six. Parent and teacher resources available.

Word-of-the-day (gr. 6-12)
http://word.parlez.com/

A detailed definition of a daily word using anecdotes, origins, quotes and current events. Archive of past words and a free subscription are available.

Young Authors Workshop (gr. 4-7)
http://www.planet.eon.net/~bplaroch/index.html

This website provides students with links to online resources that will take them step by step through the writing process. The steps in this process are those used in Writer's Workshop. The pages are designed for use by an individual student or small group of students working on a project.

Math

About Today's Date (gr. K-12) (Teachers)
http://www.nottingham.ac.uk/education/number/

Find out about the numbers used in today's date. Based on the book *Numbers: Facts, Figures and Fiction* published by Cambridge University Press. Here's a good Math warmup: Go to the board and write the digit(s) of today's date and have students try and write all the facts associated with it. They'll be surprised when you write down the facts that you know, now that you've read this page!

A+ Math (gr. 2-7)
http://aplusmath.com/

Create and print out flashcards, worksheets, interactive Math games.

Absurd Math (gr. 5-8)
http://www.learningwave.com/abmath

Here's an interactive mathematical problem solving game series that will challenge and appeal to students. Lots of hidden clues. Students must read carefully and use their mathematical skill and knowledge to solve the adventures. Answers are available to teachers and parents by e-mail.

Calculator Lessons (gr. 2-16)
http://education.casio.com/calculat1.htm

Calculator activity lessons with teacher answers from Casio. Activities for elementary, middle school, Algebra I and II, as well as Graphing and Calculus.

Cool Math (gr. 3-12)
http://www.coolmath.com/home.htm

An amusement park of Mathematics! This website certainly is fun and educational. Check out the Lissajous Lab for something cool. Try out the links to Algebra, Tessellations, Geometry, Calculus, Fractal Gallery and Fractal of the Day, Trigonometry, Fun with Numbers, How to Succeed in Math and links to great sites and resources. Highly recommended.

Elementary Problem of the Week (gr. 3-6)
http://mathforum.com/elempow/

Problems, problems and solutions. Give students the Math problem and have them work on it during the week. Vote on the best answer and explanation and submit the answer by the weekly deadline. Names of students and teams submitting correct responses are posted on the solution pages, and each week several well-written student solutions are highlighted. In addition, special certificates are mailed to individuals and teams as they achieve the 10, 20, 30, and 40 point milestones. At the end of the school year (end of May) additional certificates are awarded for school participation. Highly recommended.

Escape From Knab (gr. 6-11)
http://www.escapefromknab.com/

Escape from Knab is an educational simulation using Math concepts on the fictitious planet of Knab. Visitors soon discover the results of their actions and decisions. Lessons and answers for teachers are available.

Geometry Problem of the Week (gr. 5-8)
http://mathforum.com/geopow/

Every week a different geometry problem for your students to solve. Have your students share these problems and their solutions with you and make sure they can explain the reasoning behind their solutions. If there is no explanation, the solution will be politely refused. (My students quickly found this out!)

Grade 5/6 Finch Math Problem of the Week (gr. 3-6)
http://www.mbnet.mb.ca/~jfinch/math.html

Math problems with answers for each week of the school year. There is one problem a week for both grades 3 and 4 and for grades 5 and 6.

Interactive Mathematics Miscellany and Puzzles (gr. 5-16)
http://www.cut-the-knot.com/

Intriguing puzzles, information, quotations and problems all about Math.

The Little Math Puzzle Contest (gr. 5-10)
http://www.microtec.net/academy/mathpuzzle/

A weekly Math contest designed for students in grades 5-10. An archive of past problems is available. Includes interactive feature for over 400 problems. Just type in the answer and find out immediately if it's the correct one.

Mathematics Problem of the Week Contest Page (gr. 4-16)
http://www.olemiss.edu/mathed/problem.htm
http://pegasus.cc.ucf.edu/~mathed/problem.html

These sites present six weekly Mathematics problem contests sponsored by the Mathematics Education Programs of the University of Central Florida and the University of Mississippi and the CASIO Classroom. There is the Elementary Brain Teaser (grades 6 and under), Middle School Madness (grades 6-8), High School Challenge (grades 9-12), Problem of the Week (open to all), Geometry Gambit (grades 6-12) and Algebra in Action Contests (grades 6-12). Great calculator prizes from Casio are given weekly. Winners are selected randomly. All students with the correct solutions have their names, schools and locations displayed on the site. (You can substitute student names with the classroom teacher's name). Archives to previous problems are also available.

Math Brain Teasers (gr. 3-7)
http://www.eduplace.com/math/brain/

This site from the Houghton Mifflin Company has a wonderful collection of Math brain teasers divided by grades 3-4, 5-6 and 7+. Each week brain teasers are posted and the solutions appear the following week. Strategies are given to help solve the problem in the form of hints. An archive is also available.

Math for Kids (gr. 3-6)
http://tqjunior.advanced.org/4471

Designed by two fourth graders for fourth graders who want to sharpen their math problem-solving skills. Includes word problems and how to solve them.

Math Glossary (gr. 1-8)
http://www.hbschool.com/glossary/math/

An animated, wonderfully illustrated, very easy to use math glossary from Harcourt School Publishers. All you have to do is click on the grade and the term, and up comes the definition. A fantastic resource! Highly recommended!

Math Goodies (gr. 4-9)
http://mathgoodies.com/

Over 400 pages of Math activities. Includes interactive lessons, crossword and search puzzles, chat boards, image library, educational links, articles, newsletter, homework area for students and more. Highly recommended!

Math On Line (gr. 5-12)
http://www.mccc.edu/~kelld/page100.html

Here you can read tips on Studying Math, and take the interactive quizzes covering major concepts in Math. The quizzes are highly recommended.

Math Puzzle Corner (gr. 3-12)
http://www.aimsedu.org

This site offers work sheets with monthly puzzles to improve Math skills. These highly motivational puzzles will definitely stimulate student thinking. There is also an archive of puzzles from past years. Highly recommended.

Math Stories (gr. 1-8)
http://www.mathstories.com/

Download and print over 4,000 Math problems for your students.

Maths Online (gr. 9-16)
http://www.univie.ac.at/future.media/moe/

The goal of this website is to create a novel style of interactive learning material for the study of Math. It accomplishes this with multimedia learning units on Mathematical subjects, interactive tests, over 60 online tools and links to Mathematical topics and collections.

Mathsphere (gr. 1-6)
http://www.mathsphere.co.uk/

Download over 100 Math sheets including a printable Mathematics dictionary.

Mathematics Lessons That Are Fun (gr. 2-12)
http://math.rice.edu/~lanius/Lessons/

From Algebra and Calculus to Fractals and Fractions, this site is fun.

Middle School Math Class Seasonal Problems (gr. 6-9)
http://www.fi.edu/school/math/index.html

Here's a monthly series of seasonal math problems. The pages are designed so that there are ready-made problems for each month of the school year. The problems include holidays, seasons, and sports. Many are open-ended so that children can get extra practice for standardized tests. Complete with answers.

Middle School Problem of the Week (gr. 6-9)
http://mathforum.com/midpow/

Give your grades 6-9 students these problems each week. They can be assigned as an enrichment activity or a whole class exercise. I enjoy this site because they will not accept just the answer. Explanations are needed!

National Council of Teachers of Mathematics (Teachers)
http://nctm.org/

NCTM's website offers information about publications, professional development opportunities, jobs, awards, grants and scholarships.

Problems of the Week (gr. 5-16)
http://mathforum.com/pow/

Problems in Algebra, Discrete Math, Trig and Calculus including the challenging college-level problems of Macalester College are all brought to you weekly by the educators of the Math Forum. Highly recommended.

Rick's Math Web (gr. Pre-K-12)
http://www.ricksmath.com/

Over 4,750 math problems here for learners grades Pre-K-12 who need help learning to count, write numbers, place value, addition, subtraction, multiplication, division, prime numbers, composite numbers, least common multiples, greatest common factors, factoring whole numbers and add or subtract fractions. Also includes: tips and tricks for learning different math operations and supporting worksheets for practice. Highly recommended.

Webmath (gr. K-12)
http://www.webmath.com/

This is a fantastic site for Math help. It's designed to give the K-12 student immediate help over the Internet with their Math problems. The site generates answers to specific Math questions, as entered by the student (or teacher!) What I really like about this site is that it attempts to show the student how to arrive at the answer by giving a step-by-step solution instead of just giving the answer. There are separate sections on Math for Everyone, K-8 Math (Fractions, Numbers, Using a Number Line, Ratios and Proportions, Story Problems, Calculations and more), General Math, Algebra, Graphs, Plots and Geometrical Stuff, Trigonometry and Calculus, In the Classroom (creating online quizzes). A first stop for Math. Highly recommended.

Music

CBC4Kids (gr. 4-8)
http://www.cbc4kids/ca

Great section on Music for kids. Activities include hearing a music selection and voting on the top ten, taking a quiz, young performers making a career in classical music, introduction to classical music, naming a classical tune, instruments, and links to other music sites.

Energy in the Air: Sounds of the Orchestra (gr. 2-12)
http//tqjunior.advanced.org/5116/index.htm

Take a detailed tour of the instruments of the orchestra and learn their history and what they sound like. RealPlayer plugin needed to listen to the music.

Essentials of Music (gr. 2-12)
http//www.essentialsofmusic.com/

Basic information about classical music is presented here through almost 200 excerpts from Essential Classics. Overviews of the six main periods in music history: Middle Ages, Renaissance, Baroque, Classical, Romantic and Twentieth Century; Composers: Brief biographies of nearly 70 composers, which will   bring to life the artists   and their works;   Glossary: 200 definitions with   numerous musical examples.

The Internet Piano Page (gr. 3-12)
http://www.geocities.com/Paris/3486/

This site contains various piano excerpts from the following composers Beethoven, Brahms, Chopin, Clementi, Liszt, Mendelssohn, Mozart, Rachmaninoff, Scarlatti, Schubert and Schumann. Many biographies are also given. The various well known muscial choices give a good sampling of the various talents. This site would be useful for students that are studying various composers and their styles, as well as developing an appreciation for the "classics" that your students may not have been exposed to previously. This site is best heard with Crescendo plugin available on the website.

MIDI Karaoke (gr. 5-8)
http://www.geocities.com/Broadway/3386/

Be a star! Have students learn the words to "golden oldies" for school theme days, plays, presentations in class and for school assemblies. Categories here include Television Hits, Songs From The 80's, Disco Dance and Classic Rock.

The Music Education Launch Site (gr. K-12)
http://www.talentz.com/MusicEducation/

Links to lesson plan, animated lesson plans featuring Mr. Note, interactive lesson plans and games and more. This site hits all the high notes.

Music Notes (gr. 3-12)
http://library.advanced.org/15413

Music Notes is an interactive online musical. It was developed by three high school students from Lakeland HS in New York, USA for the 1998 ThinkQuest Competition. It is designed to teach people about music using the Internet style of learning. There are five main sections to the page: Music Theory, History, Styles, Instruments, and Professions. In addition there is a comprehensive glossary, search engine, message board, guestbook and interactive games.

The Stringstuff Page (gr. 6-8)
http://www.geocities.com/Vienna/Studio/8745/

The site engages students as they research selected topics in music. It includes a World Wide Web Music activity and resource page aimed specifically at this age group. Topics include Music History, Instruments, and one miscellaneous category of fun things.

Rock and Roll Hall of Fame (gr. 6-12)
http://www.rockhall.com/

This is the website for the Rock and Roll Hall of Fame in Cleveland Ohio USA. Tour the museum, see featured exhibits, read the lyrics of the 500 songs that shaped rock and roll, meet the inductees. Rock and roll on this site.

Physical Education and Health

Games Kids Play (gr. Pre-K-8)
http://www.gameskidsplay.net/

A list of hundreds of kids games listed by category, alphabetically, and searchable by keyword. Also includes rules for playground games, and verses for jump rope rhymes. I found great versions of old favorites I use in class.

PE Central (gr. Pre-K-12) (Parents and Teachers)
http://pe.central.vt.edu/

This site bills itself as the premier website for health and physical education for teachers, parents, and students. And they're probably right! Extensive lesson plans, assessment ideas, professional information, links to websites and more.

Sports Media (gr. Pre-K-12) (Parents and Teachers)
http//www.sports-media.org/

Here's an excellent tool for Physical Education teachers, coaches, students and anyone interested in Physical Education fitness and sports. This is an interactive site that includes lesson plans, practical links for coaching, discussion forums, mailing lists, and sports pen-pals for kids. Visitors are able to find new ideas, tips, exercises, advice from colleagues and much more.

Sports Illustrated for Kids (gr. 3-8)
http://www.sikids.com/

A super site for games, sports news, challenges, trivia, polls, fantasy league.

Wall Street Sports (gr. 5-16)
http://www.wallstreetsports.com/

Here's a unique simulated sports stock market for your favorite professional athletes from auto racing, football, basketball, baseball, golf and hockey. Students learn how to manage a portfolio of stocks. Registration is free.

Science

Access Excellence (gr. 6-16)
http://www.accessexcellence.org/

The site for Health and Bioscience! Sections for Middle School Science, and High School Biology, lessons, discussions, projects, factoids. Teacher developed mystery experiments and interactive forensic mysteries.

Astronomy Picture of the Day (gr. 4-12)
http://antwrp.gsfc.nasa.gov/apod/astropix.html

Each day a different picture of the universe with a description. The Astronomy Picture of the Day archive contains the largest collection of annotated astronomical images on the Internet. These photos are out of this world!

Athena Earth and Space Science (gr. K-12)
http://athena.edu/

Track drifter buoys in the world's oceans, forecast today's space weather, investigate tropical storms viewed from space. Athena is a fantastic source of instructional material, well written lesson plans, printable student record sheets, teacher planning guides and more sorted by the following scientific topics: oceans, earth, weather and space. The project is a collaboration between (SAIC) Science Applications International Corporation, Washington State Office of the Superintendent of Public Instruction, Seattle Public Schools, Bellevue Public Schools, Northshore School District and Lake Washington School District to enhance K-12 Science curriculum and facilitate the use of powerful computational tools from the Internet. Highly recommended.

Beakman and Jax (gr. 4-8)
http://beakman.com/

This online website of the popular show and comic strips of the same name invites all to stay, play and experiment. Demos require Shockwave.

Animal Coloring Pages (gr. K– 5)
http://www.ZoomSchool.com/coloring/

Hundreds of animals in alphabetical order and by biome. Click on the animal for a coloring page and detailed description. Then print them out for your class.

Cells Alive (gr. 8-12)
http://www.cellsalive.com/

In this very colorful, visually appealing site, cells come alive. Use a biocam to see cell division in cancer cells, try techniques to enhance the microscope image, look at the creatures that cause allergies and much more.

CERES (Center for Educational Resources) (gr. K-12)
http://asd-www.larc.nasa.gov/ceres/ASDceres.html

Funded by NASA, this site contains extensive, well written lesson plans and interactive resources for the teaching of space and astronomy.

CIESE Center for Improved Engineering and Science Education (gr. K-12)
http://www.k12Science.org/

CIESE's core mission is to help K-12 teachers and administrators realize the benefits of integrating technology into the curriculum in order to more effectively engage students in learning, and improve student achievement, particularly in science and mathematics. Their unique classroom projects using real time data from the Internet will enhance any teacher's curriculum.

Color Landform Atlas Of The United States (All)
http://fermi.jhuapl.edu/states/states.html

Spectacular landform maps of every state of the United States in an easy to navigate chart. Links to satellite images, black and white maps and resources.

Discovery.com (gr. 4-12)
http://www.discovery.com/

Great site for Science resources, daily news. Links to kids and school sections. Check out the extensive list of live cams!

Earthweek A Diary of the Planet (gr. 5-12)
http://www.earthweek.com/

Earthweek author Steve Newman reports what happened under, over and on the earth every week in Adobe Acrobat PDF format. He includes Floods, Tropical Storms, Poisoning, Volcanic Eruptions, Earthquakes, Extremes and more. This is the companion website to the Earthweek published in newspapers worldwide. If you missed it in your newspaper, catch up on it here.

Educational Web Adventures (gr. 3-12)
http://www.eduweb.com/adventure.html

Design a new spacecraft, space station, turn a barren plain into a healthy prairie, manage a watershed and other Science adventures at this website.

The Exploratorium (gr. K-12)
http://www.exploratorium.edu/

A museum of science, art, and human perception in San Francisco, California USA., there are over 200 Science experiments and great resources for teachers. Learn about scale and structure from structures around the world and do the classroom activities; try the cow's eye dissection then the sheep brain dissection and find out all about memory; check out the Science Snacks,- over 100 miniature, well written and detailed science exhibits that teachers can make using common, easily available materials for their classrooms. Go to the Science Explorer for more at home experiments. Highly recommended.

First Flight (gr. 6-16)
http://www.firstflight.com/

A virtual flight school providing online flying lessons and information about private pilot training. Flying lessons here show students what it takes to fly an airplane, from pre-flight inspection to the flight itself. Good photographs illustrating lessons. Also includes real air traffic communications.

Forensic Files - Case 001! (gr. 6-12)
http://www.discoverlearning.com/forensic/docs/

Here's your chance to travel the world and become an Internet Supersleuth. This science adventure is set up like a real investigation. There are dead ends, wild goose chases and other nasty tricks to throw you off the trail of the criminals. Once you've got your evidence, head back to the lab and start using and learning scientific terms such as chromatography, DNA sequencing, antigens, antiserum and cryptography to make your case against the international criminals. Good luck Sherlock.

Frank Potter's Science Gems (gr. K-16)
http://www.sciencegems.com/

This should be your first stop for Science resources: Physical, Earth and Life Sciences, Engineering, Mathematics and Health. Resources are sorted by category, subcategory, and grade level. What makes this a great site is the detailed resource list, annotations of the links according to grade level (saves a lot of valuable search time) and updated material. Highly recommended!

Illusionworks (gr. 4-16)
http://illusionworks.com/

A very comprehensive and award winning collection of optical and sensory illusions. Detailed explanations are given. A great Science fair project idea.

Invention Dimension (gr. 4-12)
http://web.mit.edu/invent/

Find out how "White-Out" the skateboard, rollerblades and other inventions were invented. Features an inventor a week, archive, links to invention related information and resources. Have students research their favorite inventions. Read the featured inventor to your class.

MAD Labs (gr. K-12)
http://www.madsci.org/

See what a network of scientists providing Science information can do for you. Here's a site where you can ask a Scientist, search through over 15,000 answers to Science questions, locate resources, demos and ideas for Science projects, research inedible and edible experiments and take a trip through digitized images from the Visible Human Project.

NASA (gr. K-16)
http://www.nasa.gov/

The premier site for resources, links and the latest information on space.

National Earthquake Information Center (gr. 5-12)
http://neic.usgs.gov/neis/current/

Students can look up the latest information on any earthquake in the world. Print out the maps for your bulletin board and have students predict when and where the next earthquake will occur. List the last 21 earthquakes worldwide.

National Science Foundation (Teachers)
http://www.nsf.gov/

An invaluable resource for grants, awards and the latest Science information.

Netfrog The Interactive Frog Dissection
An On-Line Tutorial (gr. 7-12)
http://curry.edschool.Virginia.EDU/go/frog/

This tutorial comes complete with text, photos and movies of a frog. Just click.

Neuroscience for Kids (gr. K-12)
http://faculty.washington.edu/~chudler/neurok.html

Explore the nervous system like you've never done before. Do experiments, activities, color pages from the neuroscience coloring book, try and solve innovative puzzles and games that will stimulate your brain. Comes with detailed lesson plans. Great ideas for Science Fair projects and links to other sites. Sign up for a free Neuroscience for Kids Newsletter. You can even keep track of information you find on this site with a specially designed form which you can e-mail to yourself.

The New Scientist (gr. 8-16)
http://www.newscientist.com

Weekly Science magazine with in depth articles on events making the news in Science. Archive of back issues also available. Links to seven new Science sites each week. One innovative feature is the taking of questions from the magazine and putting them in a section called The Last Word. Also found at **http://www.last-word.com/** for grades K-12. Answers to such questions as: Why is the sky blue? Why don't penguins' feet freeze? Why do some nation's drive on the left? and others can be found here under nine categories.

Physics Demonstration Book (gr. 11-16)
http://sprott.physics.wisc.edu/demobook/intro.htm

A remarkable and wonderful online source book for Physics teachers.

Questacon (gr. K-16)
http://www.questacon.edu.au/

Questacon is Australia's National Science and Technology Centre. Here you can explore the fascinating world of Science and Technology by taking a virtual tour where you can interact with, and get your hands, minds and bodies on more than 200 exhibits, go to the Fun Centre and try some of the 500 puzzles in the Maths Centre (Shockwave plugin required) and explore illusions, Science experiments, dinosaurs and more. Highly recommended.

Science Daily Magazine (gr. 5-12)
http://www.sciencedaily.com/

Science Daily brings breaking news about the latest discoveries and hottest research projects in everything from Astrophysics to Zoology. Stories are available in magazine format and by topic and keyword search.

Science Fair Central (gr. 4-12)
(Parents and Teachers)
http://www.discoveryschool.com/sciencefaircentral/

This feature from Discovery Channel's award-winning educational website, is designed to encourage interest and participation in Science fair competitions across the country. The Science Fair Studio - the ultimate guide to Science fair preparation for students, parents and teachers. The Studio contains a comprehensive, step-by-step handbook for students, lists of great Science fair project ideas and links to online resources. It also features a bulletin board hosted by Science fair expert, Janice VanCleave, author of over 20 books on Science projects and Science fairs. Highly recommended.

ScienzFair Project Ideas (gr. 4-12)
http://members.aol.com/ScienzFair/ideas.htm

This is a fast growing and popular site for teachers and students grades 4-12 seeking Science fair projects, ideas and web references. Hundreds of ideas for Science fair projects can be found in 21 categories with links to more sites for more ideas. This site also has a search engine to look up projects by name or by keyword. Includes Science ideas for younger students. Highly recommended.

Science/Nature for Kids (gr. K-8)
http://kidscience.about.com/

Gayle Olson is the guide to the Science and Nature for Kids site at About.com. She produces a weekly, well thought out Science resource site with puzzles, projects, articles and links to other Science activities and resources.

The Science Spot (gr. 5-8)
http://kato.theramp.net/sciencespot/

The Science Spot provides great lessons, activities and ideas for middle school educators and students. Check out the Reference Desk and Kid Zone area.

Science Update and Why Is It? (gr. 4-12)
http://ehrweb.aaas.org/ehr/

Just the facts here about cutting edge Science brought to you three days a week. Your Science questions are answered twice a week in the *Why Is It?* column. Send your questions by e-mail or call 1-800-WHY-IS-IT. Archive available.

Skywatcher's Diary (gr. 5-12)
http://www.pa.msu.edu/abrams/diary.html

A monthly calendar of daily descriptions of the night sky brought to you by Abrams Planetarium, Department of Physics and Astronomy at Michigan State University. Links to pictures and to an archive of past issues.

The Weather Channel (gr. 3-12)
http://www.weather.com/

Find up to the date weather information fast.

The Yuckiest Site on the Internet (gr. K-8)
http://www.yucky.com/

Ask questions, play games, find out all about your gross and yucky body! This is a fun and educational place for finding information students want to know, but never ask teachers! There are teaching units (for grades K-2 and 3-8) that correlate with common class Science topics and contain scope and sequence charts, classroom activities, and links to related resources.

The Virtual Cell Web Page (gr. 10-12)
http://www.virtualcell.com/

This website offers a three dimensional view of an interactive journey through a typical cell. It has both a tour in which students can dissect various cell parts and a textbook which allows students to research such topics as active transport and organic chemistry.

Volcano World (gr. K-8)
http://volcano.und.nodak.edu/

The premier site for volcano information! Detailed descriptions, clickable maps of world regions and countries, photos, search engine and many more resources. In the Kids' Door section, there are links to the following activities and resources: Rocky's Adventures, Kids' Volcano Art Gallery, Volcanic School Project Ideas, Games & Fun Stuff, Legends about Volcanoes Virtual Field Trips, Schools' Volcano Homepages, Volcano World Kids' Quiz Volcano World Contest. This site erupts with information and resources!

Social Studies

50 States & Capitals (gr. 4-8)
http://www.50states.com/

A very complete list of states and state facts.

African Cam (gr. Pre-K-8)
http://www.africam.com

This is a live site that shows wild animals in their natural habitat in different areas in Africa. Includes a Pic of the Day. Next best thing to being there.

The Age of Exploration (gr. 5-12)
http://www.mariner.org/

Click on the Educational Programs link and head off to The Age of Exploration Educational Resource. This well written and very useful curriculum guide covers maritime discovery from ancient times to Captain Cook's 1768 voyage to the South Pacific. What makes this guide special is the teacher guide and the student activities. Twelve activities provide authentic hands on learning opportunities for students (and teachers!) Create a compass, astrolabe, quadrant and globes. (I hung up the globes in my classroom for a neat effect.) Activities include identifying the parts of a ship, word searches, crossword puzzles and a sea of more wealth. Highly recommended.

CIA World Fact Book (All)
http://www.odci.gov/cia/publications/factbook/

Maps and statistical data for every country in the world.

Connected Calendar (Teachers)
http://www.connectedteacher.com/

Use this site for a daily This Day in History topic or bulletin board. Contains a monthly calendar with links to related sites.

Constitution Finder (gr. 6-16)
http://www.richmond.edu/~jpjones/confinder/

An alphabetical list of constitutions and charters of countries of the world.

Early Canadiana Online (gr. 6-16)
http://www.canadiana.org/

Early Canadiana Online is a full text online collection of more than 3,000 books and pamphlets documenting Canadian history from the first European contact to the late 19th century. You can view the original pages on the screen. The collection is particularly strong in literature, women's history, native studies, travel and exploration, and the history of French Canada.

Education Calendar & WWW Sites (Parents and Teachers)
http://home.earthlink.net/~mediadesigns/Index.html

A monthly calendar integrating websites with themes associated with special days of the month. Information is nicely displayed in a table.

Educational Web Adventures (gr. 4-12)
http://www.eduweb.com/adventure.html

Travel back in time to the Renaissance and explore Leonardo da Vinci's workshop in search of clues; learn about the people and Geography of the Ecuadorian Amazon; go undercover to Asia to expose the illegal trade in tiger parts. They're all great adventures accessed from this site.

Encyclopedia Mythica (gr. 5-12)
http://www.pantheon.org/

Over 5,700 definitions of gods and goddesses, mythology, folklore, legends, an image gallery and more. A great source of information for Social Studies and Language Arts projects. Browse or search the site for information. Assign a god, goddess, legendary creature or monster for your students to research and write up. Have them advertise a festival and create a brochure or poster for it.

Excite Travel (gr. 3-16)
http://travel.excite.com/

A must site for planning trips and doing research on cities and countries worldwide. Browse or search over 14,000 destinations. Have students take a trip and plan the route to take by listing some of the places that they will see. Make travel brochures or multimedia presentations using this information here.

GeoNet Game (gr. 4-12)
http://www.eduplace.com/geo/indexhi.html

How well do your students know the Geography of the United States of America? They've got 2 hours to find out! The game questions are organized according to the national geography standards. They've been designed to help children think geographically and to help them build a global context for the information they learn. There are some easy and hard questions. Try it out.

The History Channel (gr. 4-16)
http://www.historychannel.com/

Make History come alive with the resources on this site. Have students find out what happened this day in History. Check out the Great Speeches section and hear the great speeches of the world. Search any topic in History.

How Far Is It (gr. 4-16)
http://www.indo.com/distance/

Calculate the distance between two places. Students could find the distance between their home and any other place in the world and see it visually on a map. Answers are returned under the heading "as the crow flies" in miles, kilometers, nautical miles with latitude and longitude of both places.

A Hypertext on American History (gr. 6-12)
http://odur.let.rug.nl/~usa/

A hypertext on American History from the colonial period to the present.

Lives, The Biography Resource (Teachers)
http://amillionlives.com/

Lives is one of the largest guides to biography resources on the Web, with annotated links to thousands of sites including biographies, journals, diaries, oral histories, memoirs, correspondence, biography collections, and more.

Lonely Planet Destinations Guide (Teachers)
http://www.lonelyplanet.com/dest/

A great place to quickly find detailed facts on any country in the world.

Maps (All)
http://www.mapquest.com/

An amazing resource that will allow you to make a map of your own address. Have students plan a trip to the local library, mall, school, relatives or to a different city and country. Worldwide maps, travel guides and driving directions in the US, Canada and Europe are all here.

Map Viewer (ALL)
http://pubweb.parc.xerox.com/map

This map viewer from Xerox allows the user to zoom in on any part of a world map. Have students zoom in on their own location.

Mr. Donn's Pages (gr. 4-8) (Teachers)
http://members.aol.com/donnandlee/SiteIndex.html

One of the best sources of information, lesson plans, units, and simulations for teaching Social Studies on the Internet. Even if you don't teach Social Studies, there are great links to resources for any K-12 teacher. Highly recommended.

Mr. Dowling's Electronic Passport (gr. 4-6) (Parents and Teachers)
http://www.mrdowling.com/

A great place to plan your Social Studies units. Includes lesson plans, unit tests, study guides. Well laid out, attractive site. Highly recommended.

Name Search (ALL)
http://www.census.gov/genealogy/www/

How common is your first or last name? Find out here. Just click on the Frequently Occurring First Names and Surnames From the 1990 Census link.

National Geographic.com (All)
http://www.nationalgeographic.com/

The companion website to the well known magazine. Great educational resources, printable lesson plans, units, blank maps and stunning photographs.

Our TimeLines (Parents and Teachers)
http://www.ourtimelines.com/

Create your own personalized timeline for you and your students. You can also create timelines for anyone else you choose and see how they fit into History. It really gives you a different perspective on life.

Terraserver (gr. 4-12)
http://terraserver.microsoft.com/

An easy to use site to find satellite photos worldwide.

The World Wide Holiday and Festival Page (All)
http://www.holidayfestival.com/

Find out holidays and festivals world wide on this site. Great resource for multi-cultural projects. Searchable by country, religion, month.

Those Were The Days (gr. 5-12)
http://www.440.com/twtd/today.html

A very comprehensive listing about the events behind today's date. One event is highlighted in detail. Contains an archive of past events and a search engine.

United Nations Cyber SchoolBus (gr. 2-12)
http://www.un.org/Pubs/CyberSchoolBus/

An educational and fun site which teaches students about global issues. Activities include interactive quizzes on flags, Geography and projects.

World Time (ALL)
http://www.worldtime.com/

See the view of the earth and find out where the sun is shining. You can also click on a country of the world to see what if it's still night or day.

Special Education

The Council For Exceptional Children (CEC) (Parents and Teachers)
http://www.cec.sped.org/

The Council for Exceptional Children (CEC) is the largest international professional organization dedicated to improving educational outcomes for individuals with exceptionalities, students with disabilities, and/or the gifted. Links here to resources, publications, articles and discussion forums.

American Sign Language (gr. 4-16)
http://where.com/scott.net/asl/

This site is designed to teach basic American Sign Language. Letters and words are represented with pictures of real hands. This site will also convert your words into sign language and quiz you!

EASI Equal Access to Software and Information (Parents and Teachers)
http://www.rit.edu/~easi/

EASI's mission is to serve as a resource to the education community by providing information and guidance in the area of access-to-information technologies by individuals with disabilities. This website does this and more.

Gifted Resources Home Page (Parents and Teachers)
http://www.eskimo.com/~user/kids.html

This site contains links to online gifted resources, enrichment programs, talent searches, summer programs, gifted mailing lists and early acceptance programs. There are also links to 4+ years of TAG-L mailing list archives, and contact information for many local gifted and government associations.

LD Online (Parents and Teachers)
http://www.ldonline.org/

Expert tips for parents and teachers of children with learning disabilities. Articles on what's new, in depth reports, bulletin board, chats and a newsletter.

National Association for Gifted Children (Parents and Teachers)
http://www.nagc.org/

Keep in touch with the latest gifted program standards, legislation, conventions, parent and teacher programs.

Special Education (Parents and Teachers)
http://specialed.about.com/education/specialed/mbody.htm

A lot of useful links, articles and information from this About.com guide.

Technology

GrafX Design (gr. 5-12)
http://www.grafx-design.com/

Click on the Tutorials link and head off to easy to follow lessons for well known paint programs such as *ADOBE;s Photoshop, JASC's Paint Shop Pro* and *Corel DRAW*.   There are also general and animated gif tutorials.

GraphicsDEN (gr. 6-16) (Teachers)
http://www.actden.com/grap_den/index.htm

The GraphicsDen has seven step-by-step lessons that will teach you how to use Paint Shop Pro to create unique digital art. Each lesson takes you from start to finish of a digital project. You can follow the step-by-step instructions to complete a similar project. Links to other completed projects.

Technology Coordinators Survival Kit (Teachers)
http://www.sccs.santacruz.k12.ca.us/instruction/edtech/
conferences/necc98

For anyone dealing with technology coordination, this site is a great resource. Access information on Tech Support, Staff Development, Communication/ Technology Coordinators, Teacher Resources, Resources for Students to Use, Internet Scavenger Hunts, Online Projects, Acceptable Use Policies, Technology Use Plans Sample Grants, Professional Development Models, Job Descriptions and more. Highly recommended.

Television Production (gr. 9-16) (Teachers)
http://www.cybercollege.com/tvp_ind.htm

Seventy modules, over 500 color illustrations and assigned readings on television production. Includes modules on TV production overview, color video quality, video camera production, composition and graphics, lighting, audio, video recording, editing, producing/directing, news/documentaries, legal, ethical issues and non-broadcast video as well as quizzes for students.

Resources and References

The Amazing Picture Machine (gr. 3-16)
http://www.ncrtec.org/picture.htm

From the North Central Regional Educational Laboratory comes this picture search engine. Enter a keyword and up comes a link to the picture. Lessons on using pictures and search tips also available.

American Journalism Newslink AJR (ALL)
http://ajr.newslink.org/

Over 18,000 links to major world, national and local newspapers, magazines, broadcasters and news services worldwide. Also includes top sites, search engines and articles on journalism. Students can find up-to-date (in some cases hourly) information on news stories. Invaluable source for research on local to world stories from different perspectives. Highly recommended!

Ask An Expert (ALL)
http://askanexpert.com/

With 14 categories and hundreds of people to choose from, students and teachers are able to find experts to answer their questions from an artificial intelligence expert to facts about zoo keeping. A very kid friendly site.

Bartleby.com (ALL)
http://www.bartleby.com/

Columbia Encyclopedia, The American Dictionary, Roget's II:The New Thesaurus, American Heritage Book of English Usage, Simpson's Contemporary Quotations, Bartlett's Familiar Quotations, Oxford Shakespeare and Gray's Anatomy are all here, online.

The Best Information on the Net (Teachers)
http://library.sau.edu/bestinfo/

An information packed source for every librarian and teacher. Sites are searchable and a table visually organizes the many links. Updated regularly.

Britannica.com (ALL)
http://www.britannica.com/

Britannica.com includes the complete, updated *Encyclopædia Britannica*, the oldest and largest general reference in the English language. Selected articles from more than 70 of the world's top magazines including *Newsweek*, *Discover*, and *The Economist* provide additional feature and current-events coverage. There are links to more than 125,000 sites, and you can also search the text of more than 100 million Web pages to find more information.

Calculator.com (gr. 5-16)
http://www.calculator.com/

Find free access to online calculators to help you solve problems and answer questions in the home, office, and school. There are calculators for finance, business, and science. There are ones for cooking, hobbies, and health. Some solve problems, some satisfy curiosity, and some just for fun. All put the answer easily within your reach.

Daily Motivator (Parents and Teachers)
http://greatday.com/

On those days where you or your students need some motivation, check out this site for daily inspirational sayings. A good way to start the day is to read them out to your students before classes begin. An archive of over 1,000 motivators can also be browsed. Highly recommended.

Digital Librarian (Parents and Teachers)
http://www.digital-librarian.com/

An extensive list of sites maintained and regularly updated by librarian Margaret Vail Anderson.

Encarta Lesson Collection (All)

http://encarta.msn.com/

A gateway to 16,000 articles, multimedia, dictionary, world atlas and other resources for students, parents and teachers. This is the online version of the Encarta encyclopedia. It's a great place for students to start a research project. Very easy to navigate and read. Highly recommended!

Educational Software (Teachers)

There are a number of sites that contain large education software sections. Here is a listing of some of the popular ones:

Allen's WinApps List

http://winappslist.com/

CNET Download.Com

http://download.cnet.com/downloads/

Educational Software Cooperative

http://www.edu-soft.org/index.shtml

Freeware32.Com

http://freeware32.efront.com/file/gedu1.htm

M&M Software

http://www.mm-soft.com/

SoftSeek

http://softseek.zdnet.com/Education_and_Science/

TUCOWS

http://www.tucows.com/

Winfiles.Com

http://winfiles.cnet.com/apps/98/edutools.html

ZDNet's Software Library
http://www.zdnet.com/downloads/home.html

EDSITEment (gr. 6-16) (Parents and Teachers)
http://edsitement.neh.gov/

EDSITEment is a gateway for teachers, students, and parents searching for high-quality material on the Internet in the subject areas of Literature and Language Arts, Foreign Languages, Art and Culture, and History and Social Studies. Includes online lesson plans, reference section and teacher lounge.

Education 4 Kids (gr. K-12)
http://edu4kids.com/

An interactive flashcard program that will test Math, money, time, facts, alphabet, vocabulary, US presidents, US Geography and table of elements.

Ex Libris (Teachers)
http://marylaine.com/exlibris/

This weekly e-zine from Marylaine Block (creator of Best Information on the Net), offers 2-3 short articles every Friday on information, search tips, reference, the Internet in libraries, page design, and links to her other sites.

Free Stuff For Teachers

There are a number of sites that contain descriptions and links to free stuff for teachers. Here is a partial listing of some of them:

Free Stuff For Canadian Teachers
http://www.thecanadianTeacher.com/

Freebies
http://freebies.about.com/

Teacher Freebies
http://teacherfreebies.com/

Funbrain (gr. K-12) (Parents and Teachers)
http://www.funbrain.com

There are separate sections here for kids, parents and teachers. Teachers can create review material for their students and give paperless quizzes to their classes. The Quiz Lab automatically grades the quizzes and e-mails the results to you. There is an online gradebook where teachers can check to see who has taken a test and which test they have taken. You can also access thousands of assessment quizzes written by other teachers. Teachers can have students write their own review material and post it. This is also a fun site with many, many educational games organized by subject and grade levels to review class material. Registration is required (free) to access the Quiz Lab. Highly recommended.

How Stuff Works (ALL)
http://www.howstuffworks.com/

Here's a great place to come to learn about how things work in the world around you. Have you ever wondered how the engine in your car works or what makes the inside of your refrigerator cold? Then How Stuff Works is the place for you! Categories include: Automotive, Computers, Food, Health, Holiday, Money, Music, Sports, Weather and more. There is also a sign up for a newsletter to get the latest news. Never be stumped by your kids again!

Info Zone Research Skills Area (Teachers)
http://www.assd.winnipeg.mb.ca/infozone/

If you're wondering about something, seeking information, choosing information, connecting useful information you have found, producing information of your own in a new form and judging the entire process and your product, then click on these links by librarian Margaret Stimson.

Kindergarten Kafe (Teachers)
http://members.aol.com/charlenewp/kkafe.htm

A newsletter filled with great ideas for Kindergarten teachers.

KidsConnect (gr. K-12)
http://www.ala.org/ICONN/kidsconn.html

KidsConnect is a question-answering, help and referral service for K-12 students on the Internet. School library media specialists from throughout the world collaborate on KidsConnect to provide direct assistance to any student K-12 who is looking for resources for school or personal interests. Through e-mail, students contact the main KidsConnect address **AskKC@ala.org** and will receive a message from a volunteer library media specialist with assistance within two school days.

The Library of Congress (ALL)
http://www.loc.gov/

Library of Congress in Washington, D.C., the largest library in the world and the nation's library. Click on America's Library: New Site for Kids/Families.

Life Magazine Online (gr. 6-12)
http://www.lifemag.com/Life/

Great daily photos and stories from the past. Back issues of the Picture of the Day and links to This Day in Life and the Century's Best Pictures.

The Math Forum (gr. K-16)
(Parents and Teachers)
http://forum.swarthmore.edu/

One of the longest running Math resource areas on the Internet! This is the first place I go for questions my students ask me about Math! You can search for Math subjects or browse the Internet Mathematics Library or for a specific stumper, Ask Dr. Math. Sections on Discussion Groups, Forum Showcase, Internet Newsletter, Problems of the Week, Teacher2Teacher, Web Units and Lessons, Math Resources by Subject, Math Education, Key Issues in Math, K-12, College and Advanced Math and Innovations and Concerns. Highly recommended.

Measure 4 Measure (gr. 5-16) (Parents and Teachers)
http://www.wolinskyweb.com/measure.htm

A well researched collection of interactive sites on the Web that estimate, calculate, evaluate or translate. In other words, they do the work for you.

The Mental Edge (gr. 3-12)
http://www.learningshortcuts.com/

The site contains a collection of more than 1,900 interactive review tests for English, Mathematics, Science, Social Studies, ACT/SAT and GED exams. The reviews are coordinated with all major textbooks and match day-to-day class activities. They are designed to help students get higher test scores and help them prepare for tests in less time. Great site for reviewing lessons.

Museums on the World Wide Web (ALL)
http://www.icom.org/vlmp/

A very extensive searchable list of museums, galleries and archives on the World Wide Web. Check and see what is online where you live.

Newspaper Lesson Plans (Teachers)

There are a number of web companion sites of major newspapers that contain daily lesson plans of the news for teachers. Here are some of them:

The New York Times Learning Network (gr. 3-12)
http://www.nytimes.com/learning/

Toronto Star Connection (gr. 6-12)
http://www.thestar.com/classroom/index.html

USA Today Education (gr. 6-12)
http://www.usatoday.com/educate/home.htm

Pics4Learning (gr. 3-12)
http://pics.tech4learning.com/pics/index.htm

Here's a copyright-friendly image library for teachers and students. The Pics4Learning collection consists of thousands of images that have been donated by students, teachers, and amateur photographers. Permission has been granted for teachers and students to use all of the images donated to the Pics4Learning collection. Links to other copyright-friendly image sites.

Quia (gr. 1-16)
http://www.quia.com

Quia is the short form for Quintessential Instructional Archive. This site offers teachers and services a number of great activities. There is a directory of thousands of online games and quizzes in over 40 subject areas. Templates are available for creating nine different types of online games, including flashcards, matching, concentration (memory), word search, hangman, challenge board, and rags to riches (a quiz-show style trivia game). There are tools for creating online quizzes, quiz administration and reporting tools and free teacher home pages. Highly recommended.

Refdesk (gr. 5-12) (Parents and Teachers)
http://www.refdesk.com/

One of the most comprehensive reference sites around! Covers an extensive list of topics, easy to navigate, and easy to read the wealth of information.

Research-It (gr. 5-16)
http://www.itools.com/research-it/

A handy one stop research site for looking up currency conversions, quotations, maps, area codes, stock market quotes, a thesaurus, rhyming words, anagram creator and more. Give students currency problems to solve, quotations to find, rhymes for their poems or French verbs to conjugate.

RHL School (gr. 4-6)
http://www.rhlschool.com

Weekly updated reading comprehension, reference skills, grammar lessons, computation and problem solving worksheets for teachers and parents to copy. Answer keys can be e-mailed to you or printed from the website.

SafeKids.com (gr. 3-8) SafeTeens.com (gr. 9-12)
http://www.safekids.com/ http://www.safeteens.com/

Great resource for keeping kids safe on the Internet. Kids safety rules, parent guidelines, filtering software, safe search engines, links, articles and more.

SchoolGrants (Parents and Teachers)
http://www.schoolgrants.org/

SchoolGrants offers K-12 teachers and administrators a one-stop site where they can find a myriad of federal, state, and foundation grant funding opportunities. In addition, the site features grant-writing hints and resources, links to a variety of related websites, grant and contest related news, and a message board. A free monthly e-mail newsletter is also available.

School House Rock (gr. 3-6)
(Parents and Teachers)
http://genxtvland.simplenet.com/SchoolHouseRock/index-hi.shtml

Use the catchy music and videos from this website to teach multiplication facts (0-9), grammar rules, Science and Computer facts and American History. Rate the song on the site. Print out the words and lyrics for students to read and perform skits, dances to the music. Grammar was never this much fun to learn.

School Library Journal Online (Teachers)
http://www.slj.com/

The Web companion to the School Library Journal. Contains articles, ideas, links to the best library sites and reviews on the best CD-ROMS.

Study Abroad (gr. 12-16) (Teachers)
http://www.studyabroadandwork.com

Here's a site that provides an opportunity for teachers to earn college credit when they travel, learn a language, study abroad, do sabbatical research or work-intern-volunteer USA and abroad. During the last 21 years over 15,000 teachers have enrolled.

Teacher Time Saver (Parents and Teachers)
http://members.aol.com/ggallag958/default.html/

Teacher Time Saver is a resource for elementary educators and parents. Download shareware, freeware, clipart, and worksheets to use in your classroom. Also find links to other educational sites. Click on the Teacher Idea, Activity, and Lesson Plan Page link for fantastic resources that every gr. 4-6 teacher can use and adapt. Highly recommended.

Teaching Tips (Teachers)
http://www.teachingtips.com/

Whether you're a new teacher or a veteran, teacher Anna Gregory has lots of tips to share with all teachers K-12. In well written articles, she presents information, ideas and great techniques to use in the classroom. There is an archive of current articles, Ask Anna feature and a free monthly newsletter.

TipWorld (Teachers)
http://www.topica.com/tipworld

Each business day, TipWorld's team of experts will deliver free newsletters to your in-box. Select the tips you want, fill in your e-mail address and click on the subscribe button. Preview sample newsletters before subscribing.

Tutorial World (gr. Pre-K-6)
http://www.tut-world.com/

Ready to print out worksheets for English, Math and Science for grades Pre-K-6 complete with answers.

Video Placement Worldwide (Teachers)
http://www.vpw.com/

This site offers a list of educational videos and teaching materials free to educators. Videos are catergorized by grade levels and subject areas.

A Web Resource for Teachers and Students (Teachers)
http://www.pitt.edu/~poole/

Bernie Poole has created an indexed set of links to websites that support teaching and learning K-12. The indexes are age and subject-specific and updated almost daily. I really enjoy the Thought for the Day section. It's different from other similar sites by focusing on motivational quotations for teachers and giving a personal interpretation of them. Highly recommended.

Worksheet Factory (Parents and Teachers)
http://worksheetfactory.com/

This is the best worksheet program I've had the opportunity to use. It has saved me countless hours of preparation time in Math and Language Arts. It's a very simple and easy to use software program that will make custom worksheets. Sheets can also be tailored to individual students, allowing you to meet the needs of all your students, quickly and easily Math worksheets are geared to students in grades K to 10 with all major Math concepts covered. The vocabulary program allows you to create unlimited original worksheet activities with word shapes, crosswords, word searches, decoding and matching activities, word jumbles, and more. Free trials of the programs are available from the website. Highly recommended.

You Can Handle Them All (Parents and Teachers)
http://www.disciplinehelp.com/

Over 100 different classroom behaviors are listed here in the categories of attention, power, revenge and self-confidence. Each behavior is described in detail i.e. effects on teacher, classmates and parents and what actions to take to deal with the misbehavior. Bookmark this site for the Behavior of the Day.

Fun Stuff

1-On-1 Free Basketball Game (gr. 5-16)
http://basketball-game.com/

Take on the world with this unique, free online game. Join thousands of players as they compete each week on the virtual courts. Pick a player according to 12 attributes and decide on a strategy. Innovative way of having students make decisions then seeing the causes and effects.

Bill's Games (All)
http://www.billsgames.com/

One of the earliest game sites on the Internet. I really like this site. Every game on this site is free, requires no registration to use, no Java, frames or plugins and should work with almost any web browser. Have fun!

Brainwave (gr. 5-12)
http://www.wognum.se/brainwave/

Find the deviating symbol in the ten brain scrambles and get a brainwave award. Hints are available! See how many puzzles you can solve.

Chess (gr. 3-12)
http://tqjunior.thinkquest.org/6290/index.html

Chess is a game for the new millennium that has been around for centuries. This site has something for everyone with sections on how to play, basic and advanced strategies, chess puzzles and preparing for tournament play.

Funster (gr. 5-16)
http://www.funster.com/

A free game site with no special software required. Two word games with 1,500 easier and 1,500 harder words. You need to click on the best definition for a word from the given choices. Continue to choose until you pick the correct definition or run out of time. Great place for fun vocabulary learning.

Puzzlemaker (Parents and Teachers)
http://puzzlemaker.school.discovery.com/

Here's an easy to use and fast puzzle generator. Create and print customized word search, letter tile, fallen phrase, cryptogram, number blocks, crossword and other Math puzzles. Build your own maze or print out specialty hand-drawn mazes created around holidays and classroom topics. My students really enjoyed the word search puzzles with hidden messages. A great place.

Puzzler (gr. 2-8)
http://www.fi.edu/qa96/puzzleindex.html

An archive of puzzles collected over the years by The Franklin Institute.

Riddle du Jour and Mondo Trivia (gr. 3-12)
http://www.dujour.com/

Submit the right answer to the daily riddle or to the daily trivia question and have a chance at winning a prize. A wonderful way of stimulating students early in the day or just before dismissal.   Great over the Public Address system for school wide end of the week contests. An archive of previous riddles here.

Riddler.com (Parents and Teachers)
http://www.riddler.com

Single player and multi-player concentration, scrambler, crossword puzzles , wordsearch, trivia and solitaire like games can be found on this site. Registration required. Must be at least 18 years old.

Trendy Interactive Magic (ALL)
http://trendy.org/magic/interactivemagic.shtml

An intriguing card trick and other magic tricks. Try the card trick and see if you and your students can figure it out. It had me and my students guessing for hours. Extensive links to other magic sites.

Chapter 4

Internet Projects That Really Work

"The world communications net, the all-involving linkage of electric circuitry, will grow and become more sensitive. It will also develop new modes of feedback so that communication can become dialogue instead of monologue. It will breach the wall between 'in' and 'out' of school. It will join all people everywhere."

Marshall McLuhan

With the meteoric rise in the use of the Internet and the World Wide Web in schools and classrooms, telecommunications projects have grown exponentially. There are now projects for almost every subject in the curriculum! These projects can be scavenger hunts, virtual field trips, keypals, travelling buddies, information searches, electronic publishing, simulations, asking experts, tracking nature, online expeditions and many more. Invariably, some of the projects succeed, some fail. Some are easy to do, some are difficult. Some have been notable and some have been forgettable. The notable ones remain and are often repeated because of their educational value.

As you head toward a new school year, many of you will be planning your units and lessons for your classes. Some of you may be considering taking on a telecommunications project. Whatever type of project you choose, whether it is a travelling buddy, a virtual fieldtrip or electronic publishing or any other project, the purpose is the same — we use the technology for information and to communicate. Telecommunication projects allow teachers to teach their students to find information and to communicate beyond their classrooms and schools to an amazing world that they would otherwise not be aware of. This chapter will give you some tips, tools and resources to find a notable project that you may want to do with your students and extend their learning into the world beyond their class.

Before you head off to cyberspace looking for a project, Diane Hammond, a teacher with 25 years experience and a veteran of Internet telecommunications projects, gives these guidelines to determine if a project is going to be right for you and your class:

1. Curriculum fit
What subject areas are covered?

What expectations can be met in each subject area by involvement in the project?

Will students learn about more than just technology?

If more than one subject area is covered can/should I team with another teacher in my school?

What teaching and learning activities should we undertake as a class before, during, and after the project?

2. Timeline
How long is the timeline?

How does the timeline fit with the term/semester?

What other activities will be happening that may interfere with the project?

3. Technology requirements
What does the project require? E-mail? Web-based conferencing? CUSeeMe/ Video-conferencing? Web page creation?

What applications are my students required to know for successful participation?

How many workstations will I need at a time? How do I access/book them?

What is my school's policy on student logins/personal e-mail/acceptable use?

Who can I call on for training or technical support/backup?

4. Teaching and learning activities
Does everyone in the class participate, or is the project designed for only a few students?

Will individual students contribute data, or will they work in pairs, small groups, or as a whole class?

Will students work on different parts of the project, or will they all undertake the same activities and produce similar contributions?

What different roles can be assigned to students? Group leader, proof-reader, typist, graphic artist, data-collector, data organizer, communicator, web master...?

5. Assessment

How will I assess learning?

What is the final demonstration/end product?

What assessment criteria will I use?

Where can I find sample rubrics? [Tammy Payton has developed rubrics that primary, intermediate and secondary students can use to evaluate websites at: **http://www.siec.k12.in.us/west/edu/evaltr.htm**]

How will I assess the process?

Other Things To Know Before Students Go Online

In addition to Diane's guidelines, there are some other things you should do before having students go online once you decide on a project. Treat these virtual field trips with the same amount of planning and consideration as you would a real field trip out of the class and school. Why? Because of the dynamic "anything goes" atmosphere of the Internet, there are some places that may be inappropriate for your students. As their teacher, you know what is inappropriate based on the grade and maturity level of your students and based on the rules of your school and district.

1. My "rule of thumb" for students judging whether or not a website is inappropriate is as follows: if what you are reading, viewing and or listening to would embarrass your parents, teacher, principal, minister, priest, rabbi or mullah, then you shouldn't be there. There are times however, when students do click on a link that takes them to inappropriate material. I then have students use the "5 second rule" i.e. it should take you 5 seconds to click the backspace key in your browser to get you out of there! How do I know the 5 second rule is being violated? If we're in a lab setting, a crowd starts to form around the computer monitor very quickly. If it's in the classroom, unusually high levels of interest in the computer occur!

2. Just as classes have rules, many schools and districts have policies in place such as an Internet contract, or an Acceptable Use Policy (sometimes known as an AUP). If your school has one, make sure students and parents are aware of it. Sometimes the AUP needs to be signed and kept on file in the classroom or in the lab. More information on Acceptable Use Policies can be found at:

Yahooligans Teachers Guide **http://www.yahooligans.com/tg/index.html**

K-12 Acceptable Use Policies **http://www.erehwon.com/k12aup/**

From Now On The Educational Technology Journal **http://www.fno.org/ fnomay95.html**

3. Just because it's a "virtual field trip" doesn't mean that students can ignore common safety rules such as talking and giving personal information away to strangers. To reinforce safety rules, I have invited in the past a representative from a local Internet provider to give a PowerPoint presentation on Internet safety that employs the acronym NASTE. It stands for the following:

NAME: Do not give a stranger your name
ADDRESS: Do not give a stranger your address
SCHOOL: Do not give a stranger the name of your school
TELEPHONE: Do not give a stranger your telephone number
E-MAIL: Do not give a stranger your e-mail or your parent's e-mail

For more information on keeping kids safe online, see the following sites:
SafeKids.com: **http://www.safekids.com/** for students gr. 3-8
SafeTeens.com: **http://www.safeteens.com/** for students gr. 9-12

4. Review the objectives of the lesson and the roles of each student before going online. If you're going to use a computer lab, will you need a seating plan? Are there students you need to separate before entering the lab? (It's sometimes better to deal with potential discipline problems before entering the lab, especially if the lab is in the library or another room shared with other classes). Do you have parent volunteers or friends that can help you? What happens if the computers go "down"? Have a backup plan and make sure students know what to do if the computer goes down. Follow up on what they learned once you get back to the classroom.

5. When I first started to do telecommunications projects on the Internet, my former principal Stu Cunningham gave me some great advice. He told me to always keep parents informed of what you're doing in the classroom with their child. Send home letters of permission, notes about the project, examples of Internet work. Write it up in your monthly newsletter and class calendar that goes home to parents. The last thing parents need or want are surprises!

6. There's only so much time you have in the school year to teach your curriculum. Sometimes projects seem so appealing before the start of a new school year, that teachers develop "joinitis" i.e. signing up and joing more projects than they or their class can handle. If you're a novice to the Internet, or taking on a new and challenging assignment, consider a less intensive project such as a travel buddy, or Flat Stanley or a class e-mail project. This is much better than having to "back out" of a project because of time constraints.

Where To Find Projects

The fastest way for busy educators to find suitable projects for themselves and their classes is to access project registries and databases on the Internet. Below are some recommended sites with project databases to take a look at.

Canada's SchoolNet Grassroots Program
http://www.schoolnet.ca/grassroots/

View over 3,000 GrassRoots projects by schools across Canada. Searchable by subject, grade level, province, title, keyword, postal code and theme.

CIESE Center for Improved Engineering and Science Education
http://www.k12Science.org/

Collaborative Science classroom projects using real time data from the Internet.

Cool Teaching Lessons and Units
http://169.207.3.68/~rlevine/coolunits.htm

Teacher Richard Levine has compiled a definitive list of WebQuests and Problem-Based Learning links. In addition he has included very useful links to other forms of lessons, tutorials and projects to help you build your own units. There are also some examples of sources to help students do research.

Education World
http://www.education-world.com/projects/archives/index.shtml

An extensive collection of articles, reviews and user submitted profiles about collaborative projects. Browse by subject and grade, (Pre-K-12) or submit your project to be included within this resource. Also includes helpful information about participating in and creating collaborative projects.

Innovative Teaching
http://surfaquarium.com/projects.htm

Walter McKenzie has a detailed list of Collaborative Project Guidelines, and projects categorized according to time sensitivity, ongoing projects, project collections, and completed projects. Great links to virtual field trips, a detailed list of Virtual Field Trips Guidelines and an extensive list of Webquests.

Internet Resources Telecommunication Projects
http://www.enoreo.on.ca/students/resources/list.htm

Sheila Rhodes, Student Projects Coordinator for the Education Network of Ontario, Canada has organized in a very easy to read chart, projects in 21 categories, 9 subject areas. She also includes links to other general sites.

KIDPROJ
http://www.kidlink.org/KIDPROJ/index.html

KIDPROJ is a part of KIDLINK. Teachers and youth group leaders from around the world plan activities and projects for students and other kids age 5 to 15 (gr. K-10) to take part in. Listed here are current, year round, past and soon to be announced projects.

Lightspan.com/Global SchoolNet Foundation
http://www.lightspan.com/

Follow the teacher link on the main page to Projects Registry. One of the premier places on the Internet to find an online project. Not only are projects hosted by the Global SchoolNet Foundation included here, but the database also has projects from organizations such as I*EARN, IECC, NASA, GLOBE, Academy One, TIES, Tenet, TERC, as well as countless outstanding projects conducted by classroom teachers from all over the world.

Over 600 projects are searchable and sorted by age level and by project start date. Also available is an advanced search. This search shows projects associated with curriculum area(s), technologies used, and project levels: basic (simple information exchange projects) or advanced (complex processing of data projects).

Two projects which my students have enjoyed doing over the years is the GeoGame and Newsday. GeoGame helps students learn about our world, its maps, and its people. Great resources, great fun. Newsday involves your students in international affairs with Newsday newswire. They'll create their own newspaper based on articles submitted by global student correspondents. A very well run project. I highly recommend this site as a first stop.

Loogootee Elementary West
http://www.siec.k12.in.us/~west/online/join.htm

Tammy Payton lists a number of popular projects with detailed descriptions. There are also links to great tips and resources here.

Susan Silverman Second Grade
http//comsewogue.k12.ny.us/~ssilverman/class99/index.html

There are many examples of primary (gr. K-3) collaborative projects at this site. Check out her favorites: Bunny Readers, Community of Clocks, Online Autumn, Frosty Readers and Owl Prowl. The gateway to all her work is:
http://kids-learn.org/

Teacher Resource Center Georgia Department of Education
http://www.glc.k12.ga.us/passwd/trc/

Click on the Fairs and Contests link for a description of fairs, contests, projects, academic and awards competitions, quiz bowls and honors programs categorized under 11 subject areas. Highly recommended.

Virtual Architecture's WEB HOME
http://ccwf.cc.utexas.edu/~jbharris/Virtual-Architecture/

A website designed to support and extend the book *Virtual Architecture: Designing and Directing Curriculum-Based Telecollaboration* by Judi Harris.

Keeping Up-To-Date

One of the best ways to keep up to date with the latest project announcements teaching tips, ideas, and resources, is to make use of a listserv or mailing list, electronic newsletters or e-zines. The following sites will help you do just that!

Classroom Connect's e-mail lists
http://connectedteacher.com/listServ/subscribe.asp

Classroom Connect hosts an impressive list of e-mail newsletters for teachers:
* Classroom Today Newsletter: News about Internet-related K-12 education
* Indiana Educators: News of interest to Indiana educators
* K12 Newsletters: Content from the best of all the online K-12 newsletters,
* Library Hot Five: Updates on the best the Web has to offer, from easy-to-use lesson plans to ask-an-expert lists to online curriculum
* Net-happenings: Distributes announcements about the latest Internet resources, especially education-related
* Network Newsletter: Highlights the Net's best regularly-published e-zines
* Professional Development: Read posts from educators from around the world chock full of information about conferences, staff development, and other training opportunities
* Quest Newsletter: Subscribers receive short updates with news and information about the Quest team and adventure learning projects.

Lightspan
http://www.lightspan.com/

Follow the Communication link off the Teacher page to view and subscribe to Lightspan's impressive list of the following newsletters:
* CYBERFAIR   CyberFair 2000 Discussion List
* EXPEDITIONS   Online Expeditions Discussion List
* HILITES   K-12 Collaborative Projects List
* K12OPPS   The Best Opportunities for K-12 Educators
* LOGO-L   Discussion forum of the Logo Foundation
* NETPBL   Networked Project-Based Learning
* READRECOV   Reading Recovery for 1st graders
* VIDEOCONF   Classroom Conferencing Discussion List
* WWWEDU   The World Wide Web in Education List

Ms. LeBeau's Home Page
http://www.expage.com/page/lebeaunewsletters

Sue LeBeau has put together a fine list of links to educational newsletters, bulletins, mailing lists and electronic journals.

Teachers.Net Mailring Center
http://teachersnet.com/mailrings/

Over 60 mailrings for the following categories: General Interest, Grade Levels (Pre-K-16), Special Interest, NBPTS Standards Group, Teachers.Net Special Lists, Subject Mailrings (Math, Science, Social Studies/History/Geography, Art/Arts & Crafts, Music, English Center), Project Center Classroom Projects (Pen Pals, Postcard Projects, 100 Days, Classroom Pets, Traveling Buddies), Tech Center, Career Mailrings, Language Center (ASL/Sign Language, ESL/EFL , French Teachers Spanish Teachers) and Regional Mailrings.

Teachnet.com
http://teachnet.com/

In addition to many great tips and resources on this site, Teachnet.com hosts the Teacher-2-Teacher Mailing List. This list focuses on the exchange of ideas relevant to pre-K through grade 12 classrooms. Lesson plans, teaching tips and techniques used in the classroom are the primary focus, but the discussions can be wide-ranging. You may subscribe to either T2T (the individual message list producing 30-60 messages per day) or the T2T-Digest (a compilation of messages sent out 2 or more times per day). Archives are posted on the website and are searchable. Another newsletter available here is Brainstorm-of-the-Day Newsletter: this newsletter is sent every weekday. It brings you information on the Brainstorm of the Day, articles from the website as well as book and website reviews.

Project Ideas

Challenge 2000 Multimedia Project (gr. K-12)
http://pblmm.k12.ca.us/index.html

Project based learning supported by multimedia that is practical and easy to use by teachers who are doing multimedia projects with their students. Contains information on assessment, project planning, implementation, training curriculum, project examples and links via a web circle to other similar sites.

Cybersurfari (gr. K-12)
http://cybersurfari.org/

Over the years, my students (gr. 5-8) have really enjoyed this world wide scavenger hunt. It is a year round project with a number of different starting and ending dates. It gives students an opportunity to use an Internet browser for a clear purpose, practice in using their e-mail address, develops team cooperation and reading and thinking skills. It's also a way of exploring safe hand-picked destinations throughout the Internet. The object of the game is to find and submit as many treasure codes as possible - 132 in all.

E-Mail Around the World (gr. K-12)
http://www.buddyproject.org/

A well managed, enjoyable project that has been going on for a number of years as 100th Day Activities. The goal is to send and receive a minimum of 100 e-mail messages and to visually demonstrate how far reaching our learning can be outside of our school walls. In this authentic learning activity students are motivated to strengthen Geography skills, compare and contrast similarities and differences of different cultures and environments, and to develop their communication skills. Great ideas and 100 day activity suggestions.

Educational Web Adventures (gr. 1-16)
http://www.eduweb.com/adventure.html

Interactive online adventures for teachers and students. Adventures are categorized by grade levels and subjects. In these fun and educational activities, teachers and students will discover all about Art and Art History, Science and Nature, History and Geography. Highly recommended.

ENO Music CyberFest (gr. K-12)
http://www.enoreo.on.ca/musiccyberfest/index.htm

The Music CyberFest is an on-going project administered by teacher Stephen MacKinnon and the Electronic Network of Ontario. Registrations and entries can be made at any time. Organized in 8 categories, Music teachers send in sound files of music pieces, a digitized photo or graphic, and a short paragraph of program notes describing the piece of music. The pieces are then posted on the website and given feedback.

ePals (gr. K-12)
http://www.epals.com

Here's a fantastic resource to finding classes worldwide to e-mail.

Flat Stanley (gr. K-8)
http://flatstanley.enoreo.on.ca/

A wonderful easy to do project managed by teacher Dale Hubert. In the book, Flat Stanley, by Jeff Brown, Stanley is squashed flat by a falling bulletin board. One of the many advantages is that Flat Stanley can now visit his friends by travelling in an envelope. Students make paper Flat Stanleys and begin a journal with him for a few days. Then Flat Stanley and the journal are sent to another school where students there treat Flat Stanley as a guest and complete the journal. Flat Stanley and the journal are then returned to the original sender. You never know where these Flat Stanley's can end up. One Stanley was found floating on board the Space Shuttle "Discovery", another climbed Mt. Kilimanjaro. They have been to every continent in the world, travelled millions of kilometres, and involved thousands of students.

Friends and Flags (gr. 5-12)
http//www.schoollife.net/schools/flags

Friends and Flags is a collaborative multi-cultural learning project that combines authentic language learning with cultural understanding. It encourages a strong link between the virtual and real classroom by combining the modern technology of the Internet with the traditional postal service. Partners work in learning circles of 6 countries and exchange Friends Packs, which are rich cultural packages that reflect every partner.

Great American Egg Hunt (gr. K-6)
http://www.marshall-es.marshall.k12.tn.us/jobe/

Here's a fun way for students to search for information and giving them practice navigating the Web for a purpose while collecting Easter Eggs.

Journey North (gr. K-8)
http://www.learner.org/jnorth/

A well known project on the Internet where students track wildlife migration and spring's journey north of a dozen migratory species. Students share their own field observations with classrooms across the Hemisphere. In addition, students are linked with scientists who provide their expertise directly to the classroom. Several migrations are tracked by satellite telemetry, providing live coverage of individual animals as they migrate. Registration starts in August.

MidLink Magazine (gr. 3-12)
http://www.cs.ucf.edu/~MidLink/

Ongoing year round projects designed to encourage creativity and writing.

Online Expeditions at Lightspan.com (gr. 4-12)
http://Lightspan.com/

Online Expeditions offers opportunities for students to participate in incredible real world adventures in exotic places. Site includes an online monthly newsletter, opportunities to share best practices and participate in Online Expeditions group dialogues. Expeditions offer classroom ideas, online dispatches, video, audio links, photographs, maps, glossaries, and resources.

MindsEye Monster Exchange Project (gr. K-9)
http://www.win4edu.com/minds-eye/monster/

A student draws an original monster and then communicates that drawing into words using the writing process and the writing skills taught by the teacher. The student from a cooperating school (many times another country) receives the description and uses reading comprehension skills to try to redraw the original monster. The real trick is that the redrawn is done only from reading the description. Hundreds of schools and thousands of kids have participated.

Read In! (gr. 1-10)
http://www.readin.org/

Read In! is a phenomenally successful and huge day long reading project for children ages 5-18 in grades K-12. Students across North America and around the globe gather together by modem prior to and during the Day Of the project. At predetermined times, all classes meet in a designated chat area on the Internet to discuss books they are reading, relate classroom activities, announce special guests on site, trade suggested book titles, and "speak live" to authors and other guests with whom they discuss their love of reading.

Past authors have included Robert Munsch, Judy Blume, Avi, Jan and Stan Berenstain, Bruce Coville, Phoebe Gilman and many more. This site includes lesson plans, a chart matching grade levels and authors, registration information and activities to participate in leading up to the special day.

ThinkQuest (gr. 4-12)
http://www.thinkquest.org/

ThinkQuest Contests provide a highly motivating opportunity for students and educators to work collaboratively in teams to learn as they create materials and teach others. The contests encourages them to use the Internet to create information-rich Web-based educational tools and materials. Awards are handed out across five categories: Arts & Literature, Science & Mathematics, Social Sciences, Sports & Health and Interdisciplinary. Finalists travel to the ThinkQuest Awards Weekend to compete for top prizes. Site contains a searchable library of over 2,500 entries.

Travel Buddies (gr. Pre-K-8)
http://rite.ed.qut.edu.au/oz-teachernet/

Travel buddies are a soft plush toy or puppet that travel the world as representatives of your class. Sometimes they'll travel to many locations or just to one. They have names like Moose on the Loose, Mr. Snapper, Ollie and Oscar Otter, Scully the Skunk, Woodsy Woodchuck, Diamond the Dolphin, Timber Wolf. These travel buddies come into your class, participate in class activities, go home with students, become tourists and travel on field trips. After an agreed time, the partner class returns the travel buddy or sends it off to the next school by mailing the buddy, his or her diary of events, photos, and any other souvenirs of adventures back home. While the buddy is away, you can stay in touch using e-mail. My classes have thoroughly enjoyed the visits of their travelling buddies. Check out this site more information on how to participate and integrate this project into your classroom. Other recommended sites to see how the travel buddy projects work are: teacher Nora Boekhout has done a lot of work with "travelling stuffies." Her site **CanOz Connection**, **http://www.teacherwebshelf.com/canozconnection/** contains lots of great teacher resources, guidelines and links for starting up your own project. Great resources here for teachers who bring animals and pets into their classes. I also highly recommend checking out teacher Muriel Burns' site at **http:// www.mrsburns.com\home.htm** It is a tremendous site with information on the journeys of Otters Ollie, Oscar and Odessa. Copies of their journals, albums and artwork are archived on the site.

WebQuests (gr. K-16)
http://edweb.sdsu.edu/webquest/

A WebQuest is an inquiry-oriented activity in which most or all of the information used by learners is drawn from the Web. WebQuests are designed to use learners' time well, to focus on using information rather than looking for it, and to support learners' thinking at the levels of analysis, synthesis and evaluation. The model was developed in early 1995 at San Diego State University by Bernie Dodge with Tom March. This site contains a matrix of 200 Webquests broken down by grade levels K - 3rd, 4 - 5th, Middle School, High School and Adult/College, links to a detailed source of training materials and to the WebQuests webring and other Internet Projects .

Chapter 5

Searching And Finding Information For The Busy Educator

"Teach people to surf the Internet and they can tour the world. Teach people to serve on the Internet and they can touch the world."

Prof. Harry M. Kriz

Helping Students Evaluate Information From The Internet

1) Newsgroups can be a tremendous source of quickly accessible and invaluable information. Students should be taught that newsgroup postings are from individuals. The information from some of these "experts" can be very difficult to validate and should be taken with a "grain of salt." There may be inappropriate content about sex posted in some of these newsgroups. Always check a newsgroup before letting students access them.

2) Students should be cautioned not to ask "experts" or people in a newsgroup to do their homework/project for them. Students should show to others that they have first used other sources such as library personnel, books, periodicals and interviews before asking others on the Internet about a particular subject. Failing to do this, may result in students being "flamed" (angry messages sent to them) by others.

3) Teach some essential points of media literacy. Have students ask themselves "who wrote this and why?" Is the information a company advertisement, an article from a well known magazine, newspaper, news source or a review from an individual? If it is a review, who wrote it? Was it the book's publisher, the book's author or a reader?

4) Educate students on the source of the information. Show them how to check the URL (Uniform Resource Locator) to see where the site came from. Does the URL end in .com (a commercial site); .edu (an educational site); .gov (a government site); .org (a site representing an organization).

5) Encourage students to develop the practice of looking at the date of the material. An article written two weeks ago on the impact of computers on education would be more relevant than one written twenty years ago.

Here's a suggestion for introducing search engines from George Atkins, Chair Computer Science Department Southwestern Oklahoma State University:

One of the favorite activities for most students is to do a scavenger hunt. A class of students can be organized into teams (three or four on each team seems to work best) and provided with a list of questions to be answered using Internet resources. The questions, could be directly related to topics currently being studied in class or a scavenger type activity can be used. (See Chapter Three for examples of scavenger hunts on the Internet. A project for teachers could be to find some related to their classes or courses). Usually a timed activity, with prizes to the winners, involves the class in enthusiastic competition. Another activity that has worked well with older students and teachers is to plan a trip (for a family or small school group). I've used: Two teachers and 10 students are going to New York City during the week of _____. Find the cheapest cost of the flight, ground transportation, hotel, and entertainment expense for the group to attend one Boardway and one Off-Broadway play. The hotel should be near the theaters, if possible. Another approach would be to find the least cost to do some activity; e.g., take a group to the Grand Canyon (Arizona) and spend one night camping in the canyon (fee is associated with this). The scavenger hunt/travel activities could easily be modified for almost any class. Teachers in my Internet Workshops (after 4 days of learning to use the Internet) can come up with answers for the activities listed in about 30 to 45 minutes. Less experienced groups would, of course, require longer.

Tools and Strategies

The Internet has become the engine of the information revolution. The mountain of information available on the Internet is staggering to most users. Often users are overwhelmed and frustrated when they attempt to locate Internet resources on a specific topic. To find relevant information on the Internet, users often have to sift through an enormous number of irrelevant Web pages - which helps to explain the current popularity of Web search services. These search tools help us to sift quickly through millions of Web pages in order to distill useful material. Almost instantly, Internet search tools take your search query and sort through the millions of indexed pages and present you with ones that match your topic.

A clear understanding of how search tools operate, and strategies to help formulate search queries will greatly help your chances of locating highly relevant resources on the Internet. Search tools are not all alike, in fact, searching for the same topic on several search services will return startlingly different results. These search tools have developed as a direct response to the staggering volume of information that is available online. In order to understand the diversity of potential search results you must understand the similarities and differences between the individual search tools.

Search Engines, Directories and Meta Search Engines, Expert Lists, Educational Search Engines, Newsgroup and E-Mail Discussion Search Engines, People Searching

The term "search engine" is often used as a generic term to describe search engines, directories and Meta search engines. There are distinct differences between search engines and directories that will greatly affect your search results. Even among true search engines there are key differences in how they index pages and handle your search query.

Some search engines index every word on every page, some only index the first 20 words, some only index the "home page" or go down one level, so miss large parts of deep websites. Since the Internet is growing and changing so fast, no search engine can keep up with the increasing information. So, don't give up on a search if one engine and one directory finds nothing. Be prepared to use a number of them.

Educators may want to have students do exactly the same search with 2 or more engines to show different results. Have the students count how many sites appear in the top 20 of both engines.

Here's a handy hint for students: using the "Find" function of the browser to move to the relevant section of a long document retrieved by your search helps to see why a particular page was on the list. e.g. a search on killer whales retrieved an encyclopedia chapter on whales. However, the section on killer whales itself was near the end of the chapter and would have been missed by most students as they may not have read past the first screen.

Search engines constantly scour the Web to create catalogs of Web pages. They automatically index web pages as they "spider" (move from one site to another like a spider) across the Internet. Due to the incredible number of Web pages indexed, engines often locate Internet information not listed in web directories. AltaVista **http://www.altavista.com/** is an example of a true search engine. It has a web database of over 250 million Web pages. The AltaVista search engine indexes 10 million web pages per day, so it is a good search engine for locating recently created websites that might be of interest.

In contrast to search engines, web directories are created by humans. Websites are submitted by users, and then are assigned to a relevant category in the directory. This classification of resources into categories is the greatest strength of the directories. Yahoo! **http://www.yahoo.com/** is perhaps the best known of all the Web directories. Yahoo! also has Yahooligans **http://www.yahooligans.com/,** a search tool designed for kids. Other kids search engines (for kids 7-12) are Askjeeves for Kids at: **http://www.ajkids.com**

and Kidsclick at: **http://sunsite.berkeley.edu/click** Yahoo! has over a million listings that are all classified into specific categories in its catalogue. Look Smart, **http://www.looksmart.com/** is another Web directory which shows students how to search for information according to a hierarchical organization. These sites organize a students search into a logical fashion and make them aware of hierarchies.

These listings are categorized in a far more relevant fashion than a search engine ever could accomplish. But directories like Yahoo! suffer from outdated links because directories are not constantly indexing pages.

Meta search engines combine the strengths of multiple search engines. Instead of actually performing the indexing and searching themselves, the meta search engines use other existing search engines. These meta search engines send your search query to a number of different search engines, greatly increasing the likelihood that you will receive relevant results. MetaCrawler **http://www. metacrawler.com/** and Inference Find **http://www.infind.com/**, Dogpile **http://www.dogpile.com** and Ask Jeeves **http://www.askjeeves.com** are four examples of meta search engines. MetaCrawler automatically sends your search query to the Web's biggest search engines and then collates the results. MetaCrawler further refines the results by identifying and discarding redundant URLs (the same pages repeated in results from different engines).

While most meta search engines send out your search query to one search engine at a time, Inference Find searches in parallel. Typically, meta search engines send your query to one search engine, then wait for the response before submitting your query to another search engine. After all the sequential searches are completed the results are collated. In contrast, Inference Find sends out your search query to several different search engines simultaneously. This allows Inference Find to amass your search results with greater speed than some other meta search engines. Even though Inference Find does not submit queries to as large a number of search engines as some other meta search sites, the quality and relevance of the results are still quite high.

You can customize Dogpile to use the 18 search tools you want in the order you want to search. The browser needs to accept cookies for your preferences to be recorded and retained. You can set it to also search FTP sites and newsgroups via Deja.com at the same time as your Web search.

Ask Jeeves for Kids is a very useful search engine for elementary students under the age of 12 and beginners to searching on the Internet. Ask Jeeves allows you to ask a question in plain English and, after interacting with you to confirm the question, Ask Jeeves takes you to a site selected by Ask Jeeves research staff as being an appropriate answer to the question.

Expert Lists

A number of truly incredible people, the gurus of the Internet, have given back more than they have taken from the Internet by assembling invaluable lists of resources. The Education community has its share of these gurus. Highly recommended sites for the educator are:

The About network found at: **http://about.com** consists of over 700 Guide sites neatly organized into 36 channels. The sites cover more than 50,000 subjects with over 1 million links to the best resources on the Internet.

Berit Erickson's Berit's Best Sites for Children (under 12 years of age) site found at: **http://www.beritsbest.com** is a directory of the best 1,000 high quality, safe, fun and educational sites on the Internet.

Amanda Hill's LessonPlanz site found at: **http://lessonplanz.com** is a collection of over 3,500 links to individual lesson plans and resources hand picked and reviewed by her.

Kathy Schrock's educator's page, a list of sites on the Internet for enhancing curriculum and teacher professional growth that is updated daily, can be found at: **http://school.discovery.com/schrockguide/**

Educational Search Engines

The following search engine sites are of particular value to educators searching for lesson plans, curriculum ideas and other resources for the classroom:

The Awesome Library contains 14,000 carefully reviewed resources, including the top 5 percent in education. Only resources that have been reviewed and found to be of high quality for users are included. It can be found at: **http://www.awesomelibrary.org/**

The HomeworkCentral section of bigchalk.com has more than 100,000 organized and evaluated links in over 10,000 subjects. It can be found at: **http://www.bigchalk.com/**

Education World has over 120,000 resources in their database. Many educational resources are available at this site including teaching tips and ideas: **http://www.education-world.com/**

Newsgroup and E-Mail Discussion Search Engines

Anything goes in Usenet newsgroups. These global discussion areas cover an incredible volume of daily postings ranging from the bizarre and esoteric to highly valuable information and contacts for educators and their students. Be aware that anything can and is posted in these groups. Use your professional judgment and knowledge of individual students before having them do research here. It's a good idea to preview these newsgroups ahead of time.

Deja.com's Usenet Discussion Service provides access to approximately 35,000 Usenet newsgroups. It's a wonderful tool for searching the thousands of newsgroups for a particular subject or person. Just enter the keywords in a box and Deja.com will do the rest at: **http://www.deja.com/usenet/**

LISZT is a searchable site of the largest directory of e-mail based mailing lists in the world. Over 90,000 mailing lists are catalogued here by topics or by keyword search at: **http://www.liszt.com/**

The AltaVista search engine will also search newsgroups.

People, Business Searching

Trying to find a long lost friend, relative or business on the Internet? Do you want to find someone's e-mail address, street address or phone number? These three sites can help you in your search: Yahoo! People Search found at: **http://people.yahoo.com/**   Bigfoot **http://www.bigfoot.com** AnyWho from AT&T Labs **http://www.anywho.com/** If you're trying to find someone in Canada, go to Canada 411 at: **http://canada411.sympatico.ca/**

Using Search Engines To Find The Information

The specific engineering of the search engine determines the relevancy of the search results. Most major search engines consist of three distinct parts: the spider, the index, and the search engine software. The interaction of these three parts of the search engine determines the validity of the search results. Search engines do not all operate in the same way and they are all accessing a different selection of web pages.

The spider is sometimes called the crawler, indexer, or bot (short for "robot") and is responsible for visiting web pages and building an index for the search engine. Typically, most search engines operate an army of spiders that aggressively travel the Web searching out content. Spiders visit a web page, digest the content, and follow the links to other pages within the website. The number of pages these spiders visit, and how often they visit each page depends on the specific search engine.

The spider stores whatever information it finds in the index or catalogue. In many search engines, the index contains a text-only copy of every web page the spider visited. Some search engines remove often-repeated words (like "the" or "an") or replace them with special characters in an effort to save space. This index forms the knowledge-base or database for all subsequent search queries.

The search engine software handles your search query or question, and looks for pages containing one or more of the search terms you've specified. After identifying pages that match your search terms, the software displays the matches ranked by a method that usually incorporates both the location and frequency of the search terms.

Search Strategies

Keyword and Subject Searching

In order to harness the great power of the Internet search tools, you must first understand general information locating concepts. Understanding these key concepts will help you formulate more successful searches that achieve more relevant "hits". Search engines use "keyword" searching and will link their searches to single pages. Web directories use subject searching and link their searches to whole sites. This means that engines do a better job with very specific topics and directories do better with broader subjects e.g. antibiotic resistance in bacteria vs medical research. Directories are also better to find organizations.

Keyword searching on a search engine such as Alta Vista will typically retrieve more documents than a subject classification scheme, but many of the hits will be useless to you. Keyword searching on a search engine provides the user with a greater number of documents than a subject search, but many of these pages will not be entirely relevant to your topic. Developing a comprehensive word list to use in keyword searches is central to the success of the search. Search engines typically search for exact-word matches, and separate multiterm queries to locate web pages with any of the keywords. The quality of the number of documents retrieved is sacrificed for a higher quantity of documents retrieved.

Subject searching using a category or classification arrangement such as Yahoo! will often return a high number of relevant documents, but you are limited to the URLs that the authors of the classification scheme have included. Subject based searches limit your search to a specified classification of documents, but while the quantity of resources might be limited, the quality of the documents retrieved will be higher.

To retrieve the most relevant web documents, search both search engines and web directories. A thorough search will combine the search engine approach and the subject classification approach.

Formulating a Search Strategy

To achieve the best results from your search queries you need to learn the basics of online searching. Search tools use "query operators" to define the parameters of your actual online search. Take the extra time to read the FAQ (Help and Frequently Asked Questions files) for each search tool. All search tools are not created equally and reading the instructions for each tool will assist you greatly in your searches. To properly formulate successful searches you need to understand the following concepts:

1. Boolean Searching: Search engines often allow you to include/exclude specific words ("and", "or," and "not"). These specific words are commands that link subject terms in the search request and greatly increases the relevance of the resulting documents. While some searches use actual words, others use symbols ("+" and "-" signs) for the same purpose. Boolean searching looks for relationships between different pieces of information. Boolean logic helps to streamline your search and specifies which search words or terms are included or excluded in your search.

Adding "and" or "+" narrows the scope of the search as you retrieve fewer results when both terms are present. For example, Glendale and Tillsonburg or Glendale + Tillsonburg will only return documents that contain both words. The use of "or", such as Glendale or Tillsonburg, will display documents where either Glendale or Tillsonburg appears in the text. The use of "not" and "-" also narrows the scope of the search as you retrieve fewer results when both terms must be present. The use of 'not' often means the discarding of relevant pages because they have both the term you want and the one you don't want. Glendale not Tillsonburg or Glendale - Tillsonburg will return a more limited list of documents where Glendale appears, but not Tillsonburg.

Not all search engines use Boolean searching, and those that do often use their own protocols, symbols and parameters. To see how your favorite search engines use Boolean searching, read their help of FAQ files.

2. Proximity Searching: This type of searching allows the user to specify the physical distance between the search words on the web document. This allows the user to indicate that a search word must appear close to another search word in the document, such as Glendale near Tillsonburg. Proximity searching allows the user to find words located within a certain number of characters of each other. Not all search engines use "near" in the same way. For example, AltaVista uses it to find words within ten characters of each other, while WebCrawler lets you specify the exact number of characters.

3. Wildcard Searching: This ability allows variations in the spelling of specific words in your search query. Wildcard searching also lets the user quickly search for different forms of the same word. The wildcard ability greatly speeds up a search when the user is not exactly sure how the search term is used in context on the page. Instead of doing separate searches you can combine your requests into one search parameter. For example, a wildcard search for flavo*r will find both flavour and flavor. In the same way searching for search* will find documents that contain search, searches, searched, searching and all the other possible variations.

> Although the * symbol is a near-universal wildcard character, some search engines use different characters, or no character at all. Again, read the help or FAQ files for more information.

4. Phrases: This search ability allows the user to specify that a series of words are to be treated as a phrase. The user typically indicates the words that are to be treated this way by enclosing them between double quotation marks. As previously mentioned, most search engines parse multiterm queries to find web pages with any of the keywords. A search for "Glendale High School" will return only those web documents that contain the phrase Glendale High School, and not any pages that contain the individual words.

5. Natural Language Searches: Many search engines now allow users to enter queries as standard questions, such as "Who was the 10th President of the United States?" When this question is posed to Ask Jeeves, the meta search engine returns a brief biography of John Tyler, along with related links such as that of Sherwood Forest, Tyler's home in Virginia.

Understanding your Search Results

How Search Engines Rank Web Pages: Search engines typically rank the results of a web search according to the relevance of the specific web document. The relevancy of the ranking is directly related to how frequently the keywords or phrases appear in the document. Most search engines assume that web pages containing repeated keywords or phrases are more relevant than others to the topic, and rank them higher in their list (although many try to filter out pages that overuse keywords in an attempt to "spam" search engines). Search engines also increase the relevancy ranking of documents that feature keywords near the top of a web page, or in the first few paragraphs.

Some search engines also give higher relevancy ranking to popular websites. WebCrawler uses link popularity as a key part of its ranking system. It determines which pages in its index have a great number of links leading to them, and increases the relevancy ranking of these pages. WebCrawler believes that the popularity of a site is directly related to how highly other users regard the content of that particular site. However, most Internet users quickly discover that the popular websites are not always the ones that feature the best content.

Search Tools and Strategies Resources on the Web: The following sites offer excellent reviews of the various search, meta search engines and directories.

Search Engine Watch
http://searchenginewatch.com/

Choose the Best Search Engine for Your Information Needs by Debbie Abilock
http://nuevaschool.org/~debbie/library/research/adviceengine.html

Try Debbie and Damon Abilock's NoodleQuest search strategy wizard located at: **http://www.noodletools.com/**

Finding Information on the Internet A TUTORIAL by Joe Barker
http://www.lib.berkeley.edu/TeachingLib/Guides/Internet/FindInfo. html

Best Search Tools **http://infopeople.org/src/srctools.html**
A website listing 12 search tools (subject directories, metasearch engines, and search engines) all on one page. Just pick a search tool and enter your keyword.

Kid's Search Tools **http://www.rcls.org/ksearch.htm**
This website follows the same format as the website above. There are 17 search tools for teachers and kids. Highly recommended.

The preceding information was contributed substantially by Jim Robertson. The charts on the following pages are reproduced (with minor modifications) by permission of Debbie Abilock, Librarian/Curriculum Coordinator at The Nueva School (San Francisco Bay area) California, USA. The original information is regularly updated and can be found at:
http://nuevaschool.org/~debbie/library/research/adviceengine.html

Choose The Best Search For Your Purpose

Information need	Search strategy
I need a few **good hits fast.**	Google **http://www.google.com/** returns important, relevant hits quickly with old terms; pages cached in case the site's down and weighs importance and value on others' links. Ixquick Metasearch **http://ixquick.com/** submits your search (use phrases, boolean logic, wildcards) to major search engines and displays results that are universally ranked in the top ten.
I have a general **broad academic subject** and need to explore or focus it.	Infomine **http://infomine.ucr.edu/Main.html** high-quality subject tree; librarian-selected Librarians' Index to the Internet - **http://lii.org/** Northern Lights **http://www.northernlight.com/search.html** organizes results into folders by concept Encyclopaedia Britannica **http://www.britannica.com/** provides a topic article and Web links
I have a general **popular or commercial topic** and need to explore or focus it.	Yahoo **http://www.yahoo.com** a "tree" with sites submitted by users GO **http://www.go.com/WebDir/** focuses on entertainment, recreation, leisure and lifestyle
I have **general keyword(s)** and need **help refining** my search strategy.	HotBot SuperSearch's **http://www.hotbot.com/** template helps you create a Boolean or phrase search, or limit by media type, date etc. FAST Search Advance Search template casts a **http://www.ussc.alltheweb.com/** fast, wide net. Excite **http://www.excite.com/** suggests word lists to refine your first search term. Search for more on-target results based on successful hit. Altavista **http://www.altavista.com/** suggests phrase search terms on your results page.

Information need	Search strategy
I bet this search has **been done before.**	Ask Jeeves! **http://www.askjeeves.com/** prepares answers to common questions asked in natural language. Direct Hit **http://www.directhit.com/** a "popularity engine" which ranks your hits based on other searchers' behaviors.
I need **quality, evaluated pathfinder guides** prepared by a **subject expert.**	AlphaSearch **http://www.calvin.edu/library/ as/** and WWW Virtual Library **http://vlib.org/ Overview.html** search or browse subject-organized full-text documents, databases and gateways . New Athenaeum **http://members.spree. com/athenaeum/mguide1.htm** guide to guides with reading level estimated. Argus Clearinghouse **http://www. clearinghouse.net/index.html** librarian/ academic evaluated subject guides. About.com **http://about.com/** popular commercial evaluated subject guides BUBL LINK **http://bubl.ac.uk/link/ddc. html**- organized by Dewey number (European focus)
I want to search on **often-ignored words in a phrase** (e.g. "*Vitamin A*" or "*to be or not to be*").	Infoseek **http://infoseek.go.com/** includes little words (such as a, to, be, not) in the search
I need a **pinpoint search** using a unique phrase or word.	AltaVista **http://www.altavista.com/** works best for needle-in-the-haystack search for unique word or phrase (Himalayan cat not cat). For Canadian searches use AltaVistaCanada **http://altavista.ca/**

Information need	Search strategy
I need information on a **proper name** (a place, person, or object).	AltaVista **http://www.altavista.com** and Infoseek **http://www.infoseek.com/** search with capital letters to force an exact case match on the entire word (e.g. Claude Monet and NeXT). A person search on HotBot Super-Search will retrieve the name in both reversed and normal order **http://www.hotbot.com/**
I need **biographical information**.	Biographical Dictionary **http://www.s9.com/ biography/**- quick identification of a name. Biography.com **http://www.biography.com/ search/** - database of 20,000 paragraph-length biographies. Lives **http://amillionlives.com** links to biographies, autobiographies, memoirs, diaries, letters, narratives, oral histories and collections by profession and region.
I need a **company's** Web site.	1Jump **http://www.1jump.com/** direct to company's website using company or brand name, stock ticker symbols, name of an executive or employee, geographic terms (ZIP, postal code, city name)
I need **US government** information. I need **Canadian government** information.	FedWorld **http://www.fedworld.gov/** browse government databases or websites, keyword searches on government Web pages or reports Canada Site **http://canada.gc.ca/**
I need a **virtual librarian**.	KidsConnect, **http://www.ala.org/ICONN/ AskKC.html** Internet Public Library Reference, **http://www.ipl.org/ref/QUE/ RefFormQRC.html** Debbie, **debbie@nuevaschool.org** Marilyn **mkimura@nuevaschool.org**

Information need	Search strategy
I need **hard-to-find or late-breaking information**.	Inference Find **http://www.infind.com/** a "metasearch" which queries multiple engines simultaneously; likely to pick up rare or recent information not widely indexed. YahooNews **http://dailynews.yahoo.com/** updates continuously from newswires; with full coverage of hot topics. Northern Lights Current News **http://www.northernlight.com/news.html** updates headlines, weather, and sports continuously; can search archives up to two weeks old.
I need **current information** from magazine or newspaper articles	AJR NewsLink **http://ajr.newslink.org/** links to newspapers/magazines, mainly US and Canada. News Directory **http://www.newsd.com/** links to online English language media worldwide . TotalNEWS **http://www.totalnews.com/_main.html** and Northern Light **http://www.northernlight.com/news.html** search news. UnCover **http://uncweb.carl.org/** free search of large current multidisciplinary journal index,
I need accurate, objective information on **hot topics.**	Social Issues **http://www.multnomah.lib.or.us/lib/homework/sochc.html** - Multnomah County Library's Homework Center. BIOTN **http://www.sau.edu/bestinfo/Hot/hotindex.htm** compiled by librarians at a Catholic university about controversial current events issues (e.g. gun control, censorship etc.).
I need **statistical data**.	Statistical Information **http://nuevaschool.org/~debbie/library/cur/math/stats.html** help page at Nueva.
Is there **almanac-type** information on the Internet?	Information Please **http://www.infoplease.com/** (almanac facts) CIA World Factbook . **http://www.odci.gov/cia/publications/factbook/index.html** (country facts).

Information need	Search strategy
I need **primary sources**.	Online Digital Library **http://www. digitallibrary.net/resources.asp** US focus: American Memory, **http://lcweb2. loc.gov/ammem/ammemhome.html** Ancient Greece: Perseus Project, **http://www. perseus.tufts.edu/** Early Canadiana **http:// canadiana.org/**
I need **images** and **sounds** (photos, art, designs, logos, videos, music, noises), **media types** (Java, VRML) or **file extensions** (.gif)	Amazing Picture Machine (NCREL) **http:// www.ncrtec.org/picture.htm** small, education-appropriate pictures. American Memory **http://memory.loc.gov/ ammem/collections/finder.html** US historical images and sounds; search by formats (maps, motion pictures, photos and prints, sound recordings). AltaVista Photo Finder **http://image. altavista.com/cgi-bin/avncgi** searches 17 million images, audio clips, video files from the web and private collections. HotBot: SuperSearch **http://www.hotbot. com/** template has options for media type. Columbia University's WebSEEk **http://disney.ctr.columbia.edu/webseek/** catalogues 650,000 images and videos on Web Lycos RichMedia **http://multimedia.lycos. com/** (sounds, images, videos) FAST powered Jacob Richman has compiled an list of quality picture/art sites. **http://jr.co.il/hotsites/ pictures.htm**
I need a **map**.	TIGER Map Service **http://tiger.census.gov/ cgi-bin/mapbrowse-tbl** maps for Web pages from U.S.Census National Geographic Map Machine **http://www.nationalgeographic. com/maps/index.html**- printable country, physical and political maps, star charts MapQuest **http://www.mapquest.com/** inter-active service for driving directions.

Information need	Search strategy
I need a **quotation**.	The Quotations Page **http://www. starlingtech.com/quotes/** Quoteland **http://www.quoteland.com/** Quotations Archive, **http://www.aphids.com/ quotes/index.shtml** Search Creative Quotations, Bartlett (1901) **http://www.bemorecreative.com/**
I want to get **advice and opinions** from others.	Ask Kids' Connect **http://www.ala.org/ ICONN/AskKC.html** question answering and referral by librarians . AskA+ **http://www.vrd.org/locator/ subject.html** authoritative, non-commercial experts, suitable for K-12. Pitsco's Ask an Expert **http://www. askanexpert.com/** volunteers with varying levels of expertise. Liszt **http://www.liszt.com/** catalogs.
I want notice of **new sites** as they're announced.	Scout Report Signpost **http://www.signpost. org/signpost/** reviews of new sites not yet listed on expert sites.
I've got a **good search to rerun automatically**.	Informant **http://informant.dartmouth.edu/** repeats your search, sends e-mail when hits change.Excite's NewsTracker **http://www. excite.com/Info/newstr/quickstart.html** tracks your news topic, refining search based on results Northern Light Search Alert Service **http://standard.northernlight.com/cgi- bin/cl_alert.pl** runs your search on a large database
I want to see sites **just for kids**.	KidsClick! **http://sunsite.berkeley.edu/ KidsClick!/** Yahooligans! **http://www.yahooligans.com/**

Chapter 6

Publish Or Perish...No One Knows What You've Done Until You've Told Them

"Transport of the mails, transport of the human voice, transport of flickering pictures. In this century, as in others, our highest accomplishments still have the single aim of bringing men [and women] together."

Antoine de Saint-Exupery

25 Reasons Why Every School Should Have a Website

1. A website is a showcase telling people who you are, what you and your school have done, written from your point of view. Your mission statement, vision statement mottos and school policies are there for all to see.

2. It makes connections with readers in your own school and beyond the four walls of the school building to the wider world community. It brings the world to your students and your students to the world.

3. Your site can offer readers an opportunity to provide instant feedback on what you've written, what the school has done and hasn't yet done. A website isn't a passive medium. It promotes active, interested and willing learners.

4. Post a map of where your school is located with your city, state/province and country. Detailed instructions ensure that no visitor will ever get lost!

5. It gives students a purpose to write. Instead of writing for themselves, their peers and their teacher and then having their work posted in the class or in the school, students can now reach a wider world audience.

6. Authors who read student book reports of their own books can now comment directly with their audience. Students quickly find out the need for accuracy, clarity and good spelling in their writings!

7.   Parents and separated parents, grandparents and relatives who live a distance away, can now stay in touch with the school and see the work of their next generation.

8.   Students can see history come alive. A timeline of your school, photos of past events, achievements, celebrations can now be made available.   Students can interview, photograph, research and write about their school.   With the cost of memory decreasing daily, there is virtually no limit to what can be stored on the website. New staff and students can now quickly learn about the school and become a part of its community.

9. Let others find and connect with you. Once you have a web page, magical connections take place! A unit for example on Japan that your class has done now brings a reply from a Japanese educator requesting pen pals and for students learning English for the first time. Other educators read your request for electronic pen pals and offer to match up their students with yours. Students begin to write to other students in places they never knew existed. The unknown world becomes more personalized and students find that this world community is a small, fragile and precious one.

10.   Links to sites that are appropriate for staff and students can be added to your web pages. This provides a focus for students when they are online. Subject based curriculum pages with helpful links are ideal for homework and independent study. This saves staff and students time from searching for sites.

11.   Elementary and secondary schools can highlight their events by adding banners and marquees to their websites. The community can be informed on the latest fundraisers, musical, sporting and academic events being held. Web pages help foster collaboration among students, teachers, parents and the world wide community.

12.   Electronic portfolios provide a record of students' works. It also gives students a digital copy to refer to in upcoming years if they've lost their original projects. Students are provided with models to follow, to improve upon. Teachers can now quickly and easily refer to former, present and future students' achievements online, from school, home or anywhere they have access to a computer.

13. Saves paper.   Copies of class and school newspapers, newsletters, handouts can be reduced or eliminated by the website. Students who lose or who want extra copies of newspapers now have unlimited copies from the website. Requests for copies of presentation handouts can be referred to the website. Staff too, can find those important memos and policies that may have been misplaced or lost, (without the embarrassment of asking for them again) quickly on the website.

14. Clubs. Parents can now see and read the latest club/team their child has joined, who the teacher is, what the club/team does, when it meets. Ideal way of fostering links and parental involvement. Parents have a greater tendency of helping if they know more and feel they can contribute in a useful way.

15. Keep in touch with alumni. They can be kept up to date without expensive mass mailings by referring them to the Alumni section of the website. It reinforces the student-school bond and sense of community. Great for keeping students from their elementary school in touch with their first "*alma mater*."

16. Sharing knowledge. It adds to the sum knowledge of the Internet. You're giving something back to the Internet community for others to share.

17. Online Courses. Homebound and hospitalized students can still keep up with their studies through courses online. Students can complete course requirements at their own pace. Teachers can provide links in their online courses that keep up with the latest ground breaking research and announcements. There is also great potential here for distance education. Students can take courses from teachers and experts in remote locations.

18. Yearbooks have become expensive to produce and to buy. Put it online and give every student access to a copy. The same can be done for art work. Create a virtual art gallery or museum featuring student and staff works of art.

19. Post student resumes. (One elementary student received an offer from a publisher to contribute stories to a kids Internet book. She now posts her cartoons on her personal web page to further her goal as a cartoonist.) Concerns about privacy can be alleviated through the use of first names or a file number and general e-mail address for contact information.

20. Connect a live camcorder to your site showing pictures of your school.

21. Weather. Set up a link to current weather conditions in your city.

22. Add a clock to your website with your local time.

23. Add a guestbook to your website for readers to comment on your site.

24. Post music files created by your staff and students and have them play in the background as people come to your site.

25. Have fun. Post interactive word searches and crossword puzzles, brain teasers and mazes on your website. Invite students to solve daily, weekly or monthly Math word problems or Language Arts riddles created by your students. Offer prizes or recognition for successful entries.

Where To Find Help For Creating Your Website

As an educator, there are many ideas, techniques and methods I come across that I'd love to implement in my classroom, but I just don't have the time, motivation or expertise to make it happen. I believe every educator has ways of making things happen in their classroom to enhance the learning and educational experiences of their students. One way is to ask. Ask your students if they know how to make a web page. (Don't be surprised if some of your students know how. I once assumed that my grade 2 students did not know how to e-mail, until I asked for a show of hands. Seven tiny hands went up. I was skeptical, so I asked how they got access and who they e-mailed. A lot of them said their grandparents had Internet access and showed them how to e-mail. Others told me their parents had accounts at work. Some others said their neighbours and babysitters had Internet accounts. Most told me they had e-pals in Europe, Australia, Canada, Latin America and the United States!) Students in the junior years are now creating their own web sites, whereas only a few years ago, it was the domain of computer professionals. The best three words of advice are: Ask, ask, ask!

10 Tips to Help You Develop Your Web Page:

1. Ask the students in your class. If your students don't know how to make web pages, they may know someone who does. It may be a parent, relative, neighbor.

2. Ask other students in the school. There may be a number of students in grades 6-8 that may already have their own web pages posted on the Internet.

3. Post wanted posters in your school and community looking for volunteers.

4. Send notices home for volunteers in your class and school newsletters.

5. Contact your local high school and community college and university for volunteers. Most schools have a co-op program or a community service component to their program.

6. Ask your computer guru on staff or in a neighboring school or your computer consultant at the district office for help or leads.

7. Contact a local Internet provider, your cable company or your phone company for volunteers or people who may do it for a discount or free, for a school.

8. If you want to learn how to create a web page on your own, you can take a course from a computer training institute, a community college or university.

9. Go to your library, bookstore or to an online bookstore and read a book on beginners' HTML (Hyper Text Markup Language) on creating a web page. Here are some virtual bookstores to browse for books:

Amazon.com **http://amazon.com/**

Barnes and Noble **http://www.barnesandnoble.com/**

Chapters.ca **http://www.chapters.ca/**

10. Use the Internet! The Internet has a number of unique resources for helping anyone with their web page. These sites provide tutorials from people and institutions who have shared their expertise with the Internet community. The following Internet resources will help you with your website.

Beginning HTLM
http://htmlgoodies.earthweb.com/

One of the Internet's most popular stops for information on HTML and other mark-up languages. Goodies contains hundreds of unique tutorials for HTML, XML, SGML and DHTML as well as one of the Web's most comprehensive repositories for JavaScript and other scripting languages. Well written and easy to follow tutorials on all aspects of HTML from the basics to advanced levels. Download section contains a listing of freeware and shareware that both new and experienced programmers can use to write scripts, create web pages, and enhance PC performance. Updated weekly.

Center for Improved Engineering and Science Education CIESE
http://www.k12science.org/

Click on the link to Net Tools. This page lists resources for teachers building school webpages. Includes a dozen places to host your website, graphics, online calendars and group management tools, free online bookmarking, free web based e-mail and links to online courses and tutorials.

Hazel's Homepage
http://www.marshall-es.marshall.k12.tn.us/jobe/index.html

In Hazel Jobe's Web Page Design section, she offers suggestions as to what you should do before you make your own webpage. She has information on guidelines, resources, child safety and Acceptable Use Policies, free home pages, HTML editors, code and HTML Tutorials. A good place to start.

Mrs. Seagraves' QUEST Class
http://www.geocities.com/Athens/Atrium/5924/index.html

Teacher Susan Seagraves has written a very useful little section on some of the neat effects found on webpages entitled How Did We Do That. In this section she includes links to dynamic HTML, Java Scripts, Java Applets, graphic links and suggested websites to find more information.

School Web Clubs
http://supportnet.merit.edu/webclubs/index.html

This is one fantastic resource for anyone who would like to help students create or work on their school's website by creating a club or special technology projects group. It has a very extensive section on Internet Acceptable Use Policies with many references and examples from other schools and districts. Includes great ideas for web club projects with links to examples of what other schools have done. A good listing of sites that give award recognition for school websites. Also has resources on web publishing, and where to find clipart, banners, scripts, maps and other stuff. I like this resource because it's written with the student in mind. Highly recommended.

webteacher
http://www.webteacher.org/winnet/indextc.html

webTeacher was created by two teachers from Tennessee, Mike and Jo Ann Guidry, and by TECH CORPS WebMaster Wayne Kincaid, who brought together their Internet knowledge and classroom experiences to develop a training tool useful for anyone, but designed specifically for teachers. Through extensive field tests giving teachers hands-on use of the program, the tutorial was refined and enhanced to address those things which would help you to use the Internet in your classroom. A very complete web tutorial for teachers.

TEACHER TIME SAVER	http://members.aol.com/ggallag958/default.html	122
TEACHERS@WORK	http://teachers.work.co.nz/	55
TEACHING IDEAS PRIMARY TEACH	http://www.teachingideas.co.uk/	63
TEACHING TIPS	http://www.teachingtips.com/	122
TEACHING WORTH CELEBRATING	http://www.ascd.org/readingroom/edlead/9905/extwasley.html	58
TEACHNET.COM	http://teachnet.com/	134
TEACHNET.ORG	http://.teachnet.org/home/home.htm	60
TECHNOLOGY COORDINATORS SURVIVAL KIT	http://www.sccs.santacruz.k12.ca.us/instruction/edtech/conferences/necc98	112
TELEVISION PRODUCTION	http://www.cybercollege.com/tvp_ind.htm	112
TERRASERVER	http://terraserver.microsoft.com/	108
THINKQUEST	http:///thinkquest.org/	138
THOSE WERE THE DAYS	http://www.440.com/twtd/today.html	109
TIGER MAP SERVICE	http://tiger.census.gov/cgi-bin/mapbrowse-tbl	154
TIME FOR KIDS	http://timeforkids.com/	84
TIPWORLD	http://tipworld.com/	122
TORONTO STAR CLASSROOM CONNECTION	http://www.thestar.com/classroom/index.html	119
TOTAL NEWS	http://www.totalnews.com/_main.html	153
TRACKSTAR	http://trackstar.scrtec.org/	55, 74
TRAVEL BUDDIES	http://rite.ed.qut.edu.au/oz-teachernet/	139
TRAVLANG	http://www.travlang.com/	79
TRENDY INTERACTIVE MAGIC	http://trendy.org/magic/interactivemagic.shtml	125
TSL/TEFL/TESOL/ESL/EFL/ESOL	http://www.aitech.ac.jp/~iteslj/links	77
TUCOWS	http://www.tucows.com/	115
TUTORIAL WORLD	http://www.tut-world.com/	122
UNCOVER	http://uncweb.carl.org/	153
UNITED NATIONS CYBER SCHOOLBUS QUIZ QUAD	http://www.un.org/Pubs/CyberSchoolBus/	109
U.S. DEPARTMENT OF EDUCATION	http://www.ed.gov/pubs/FirstYear/	60
U.S. GOVERNMENT INFORMATION	http://www.fedworld.gov/	152
USA TODAY EDUCATION	http://www.usatoday.com/classroom/index.html	119
UTAHLINK	http://www.uen.org/utahlink	47
VIDEO PLACEMENT WORLDWIDE	http://www.vpw.com/	123
VIRTUAL ARCHITECTURE	http://ccwf.cc.utexas.edu/~jbharris/Virtual -Architecture/	132
VIRTUAL CELL WEB PAGE	http://www.virtualcell.com	103
VIRTUAL LIBRARIAN	http://www.ala.org/ICONN/AskKC.html	152
VOCABULARY TRAINING EXERCISES	http://www.vokabel.com/	79
VOCABULARY UNIVERSITY	http://www.vocabulary.com/	85
VOLCANO WORLD	http://volcano.und.nodak.edu/	103
W.C.WALKER ELEMENTARY	http://www.okaloosa.k12.fl.us/walker	64
WACKY WORLD OF WORDS	http://www.members.home.net/teachwell/	85
WALL STREET SPORTS	http://wallstreetsports.com/	94
WEATHER CHANNEL	http://www.weather.com/	102
WEBMATH	http://www.webmath.com/	91

174

Website Directory

COMPLETELY REVISED & UPDATED 2ND ED.

The Busy Educator's Guide To The World Wide Web

by Marjan Glavac BA, BEd, MA

$14.95 US $19.95 CDN

ISBN 0-9683310-1-7   200 pages

The Busy Educator's Guide To The World Wide Web

By Marjan Glavac

Foreword by Dr. Harry Wong author of The First Days Of School

Written by an educator for educators, Glavac's guide is written especially for teachers using the World Wide Web in the classroom. Parents and students will also benefit from Glavac's uncovering of real sources of content, both educational and fun for the class and for the home. This book lies flat for easy reference. Visit our website: http://www.glavac.com and sign up for The Busy Educator's Newsletter for FREE.
Find:

- hundreds of lesson plans, printable worksheets, quizzes only clicks away
- resources, tips and ideas on how to integrate the Internet into the classroom
- the site for Safety on the Net, a must for every teacher and parent
- the one mailing list every librarian should join
- how to search and find educational information using search engines designed for teachers
- 25 reasons for your school to have a web page and 10 tips to help you make one
- how to access newspapers, magazines, radio, and TV resources for FREE
- projects for teachers by teachers and where to find projects for your class

Save hours of typing in Web addresses! Order the Website Directory disk with over 500 web sites from the book. Only $3 covers disk shipping and handling. (PC format only)